Publication Design by Amanda Jane Jones
Cover photograph by Seth Smoot

weldon**owen**

415 Jackson Street, Suite 200,
San Francisco, CA 94111
Telephone: 415 291 0100
Fax: 415 291 8841
www.wopublishing.com

Weldon Owen is a division of

BONNIER

KINFOLK

SUBSCRIBE

VISIT SHOP.KINFOLKMAG.COM

FOUR VOLUMES EACH YEAR

CONTACT US

If you have any questions or comments,
email us at *info@kinfolkmag.com*

SUBSCRIPTIONS

For questions regarding your subscription,
email us at *subscribe@kinfolkmag.com*

STOCKISTS

If you would like to carry *Kinfolk*,
email us at *distribution@kinfolkmag.com*

SUBMISSIONS

Send all submissions to
submissions@kinfolkmag.com

EDITOR

To reach the editor,
please email *nathan@kinfolkmag.com*

WWW.KINFOLKMAG.COM

WELCOME

These meals, moments, and places make us who we are individually and collectively.

This is the time of year when I mark the calendar for road trips and weekend getaways, and when I start to look forward to summer. But it's also the time when I pause to enjoy the growing light in the evenings, throw open windows and doors to the spring air, and invite friends over to celebrate the change in weather.

The essays and personal stories in this volume suggest that we all might benefit from incorporating more of the things we love into our daily routines instead of saving them for the weekend or our next vacation. They focus on welcoming food, community, and simplicity into our lives as regularly as possible. As we continue to look forward to summer, let's also explore simple weekday ideas that will bring us together with the people we love and the food we enjoy more often.

Our hope is that you'll find small ways to build your community as you read of people working on their own: a design firm finding ways to eat together at the office, a married couple trying to eat breakfast together every morning, and a young family that unintentionally created their own morning ritual of breakfast and freshly pulled espresso. Meals and relationships evolve in tandem: setting a date for lunch, finding our favorite restaurants and local spots, or sharing a meal that ultimately leads to marriage These meals, moments, and places make us who we are individually and collectively. They leave sweet memories to revisit every time we return to the table.

NATHAN WILLIAMS, EDITOR OF KINFOLK MAGAZINE

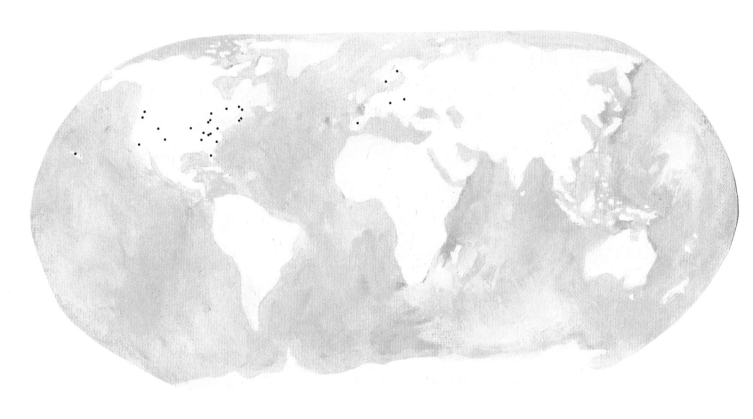

NATHAN WILLIAMS
Editor
Portland, OR

AMANDA JANE JONES
Designer
Ann Arbor, MI

ERICA MIDKIFF
Copy Editor
Birmingham, AL

JULIE POINTER
Writer
Portland, OR

KATIE STRATTON
Painter & Writer
Dayton, OH

ALPHA SMOOT
Photographer
New York, NY

LAURA DART
Photographer
Portland, OR

CARISSA GALLO
Writer & Photographer
Arlington, VA

MARJORIE TAYLOR
Cook & Writer
Beaune, France

KATHRIN KOSCHITZKI
Photographer
Munich, Germany

JESSICA COMINGORE
Photographer & Online Editor
Los Angeles, CA

OLIVIA RAE JAMES
Writer
Charleston, SC

ANDREW GALLO
Filmmaker
Arlington, VA

STEPHANIE CORRAL
Writer
Madrid, Spain

ELISE YETTON
Stylist & Writer
Nashville, TN

SETH AND KENDRA SMOOT
Photographer, Stylist
New York, NY

DAVID AND SARAH WINWARD
Writer, Florist
Salt Lake City, UT

AUSTIN GROS
Photographer
Nashville, TN

M.F. MILLER
Writer
Toronto, Canada

BRITT CHUDLEIGH
Photographer
Salt Lake City, UT

LYNDSAY REYNOLDS
Writer
New York, NY

CELINE KIM
Photographer
Toronto, Canada

LEIGH PATTERSON
Writer
Brooklyn, NY

LEO PATRONE
Photographer
Salt Lake City, UT

PAUL JEPSEN
Writer
Copenhagen, Denmark

MICHAEL MULLER
Photographer
Brooklyn, NY

ASHLEY CAMPER
Photographer
Maui, HI

BRITTANY JEPSEN
Writer
Copenhagen, Denmark

KYLE JOHNSON
Photographer
Seattle, WA

SHAUNNA NYGREN
Writer
New Mexico

AUSTIN SAILSBURY
Writer
Orlando, FL

ASHLEY HELVEY
Stylist
Seattle, WA

ANDREA GENTL
Photographer
New York, NY

ALEC VANDERBOOM
Photographer
Kansas City, MO

MOLLY WIZENBERG
Cook & Writer
Seattle, WA

MARTIN HYERS
Photographer
New York, NY

AGATHA KHISHCHENKO
Writer
Brooklyn, NY

BRANDON PETTIT
Cook
Seattle, WA

KATIE-SEARLE WILLIAMS
Sales & Writer
Portland, OR

HEATHER NAN
Photographer
Salt Lake City, UT

JOHN CULLEN
Photographer
Toronto, Canada

HILDA GRAHNAT
Photographer
Sweden

ANNIE BILANCINI
Writer
Oxford, OH

NATASHA PICKOWICZ
Writer
Montréal, Canada

YOUNG & HUNGRY
Photographers
Los Angeles, CA

JEN ALTMAN
Photographer
Asheville, NC

LILY STOCKMAN
Writer
Brookyln, NY

SAER RICHARDS
Writer
Brooklyn, NY

ASHLEY ENGLISH
Writer
Candler, NC

JENNIFER CAUSEY
Photographer
Brooklyn, NY

TRISH PAPADAKOS
Photographer & Writer
Toronto, Canada

CHRISTINA ROSALIE
Writer
Vermont

LEELA ROSS
Photographer
Portland, OR

ANNE SMOOT
Stylist
Provo, UT

FEW

ONE
ENTERTAINING FOR ONE

○

A QUIET LIFE

My solitary times fortify me to listen more clearly and to love better when I am in the presence of others.

In *Letters to a Young Poet*[1], Rainer Marie Rilke writes, "People have even made eating into something else: necessity on the one hand, excess on the other; have muddied the clarity of this need, and all the deep, simple needs in which life renews itself have become just as muddy. But the individual can make them clear for himself and live them clearly (not the individual who is dependent, but the solitary man)."

What I want is a quiet life.

I mean a life that listens: to other people, to my place, to silence. I want to notice even the smallest things, to stay immediate to my surroundings. But daily distraction can be so fragmenting, so addictive, and the kind of attentive patience I seek requires clarity of mind. To find this clearheadedness, I must make a commitment to do so—I have to say no to the constant, frenzied consumption of "needs" (more often wants and excesses), and I have to make room for the quiet, contented yes I actually desire.

I feel most acutely present when I am *away* from the noise, when my circumstances pare down all unnecessary clutter. I have experienced this fully in short parentheses in my past—living in a convent in a hilltop village, working on a remote island with scarcely 200 inhabitants, visiting my grandparents in their summer cottage on the river. These represent the simplest times, when I am completely content with nothing but words, pen and paper, the outdoors, my feet, my eyes. I return from these respites feeling soft, malleable, ready to make something good of myself.

But apart from the luxury of true time away, daily life clamors. I am folded into busyness, worrying about friends, washing the dishes, money, work, wondering what I will make of my life. It's hard to get ahold of myself in this cycle,

unless I actively venture to reassess, re-move. Even the plainest gesture can renew me—jotting a few words down (somewhere, anywhere), opening a book, taking a walk, doing jumping jacks, baking, drawing some lines, watching the trees move outside my window. In dire times I take a drive, always somewhere with unfenced expanses and wildness in which I can lie. I eat an apple; I hear the birds. I move beyond the minute scope of myself, and I am refreshed by the marvel of the osprey's nest, the river unceasing, the cows in the field.

When I am alert enough, these moments of relative aloneness overwhelm me with the freedom of choice. It is a generous gift—to choose the way I want to live, in spite of circumstance. I believe that I am daily shaping myself through my decisions, and so I make them earnestly, carefully. But I too easily fall into patterns I believe to be obligatory—habits of convenience I depend upon. I am carried away by the impulse to *keep up*, though this sentiment inspires only a perpetual state of wanting. I'd rather punctuate my days with actions turning me towards gratefulness, revitalizing my eyes to see the calm goodness already around me. If I excuse my mind from easy diversion and turn my attention to noticing what's before me—whether word, wind, or moth-wing—I find a simple quiet within me.

I love solitude, but I do not remain there forever. My solitary times fortify me to listen more clearly and to love better when I am in the presence of others. We are meant to *commune* together, which means to empathize, to relate to, to be close with. When I take the time to perceive the world as it is—and *myself* as I am—I have more empathy and gratitude for those I encounter daily, be they friends or strangers. I spend time alone to cultivate my own joy and well-being, for the sake of becoming something worthy of sharing with others.

PHOTOGRAPHS BY LAURA DART
WORDS BY JULIE POINTER

People have even made eating into something else: necessity on the one hand, excess on the other; have muddied the clarity of this need, and all the deep, simple needs in which life renews itself have become just as muddy. But the individual can make them clear for himself and live them clearly (not the individual who is dependent, but the solitary man).[1]

RAINER MARIE RILKE, LETTERS TO A YOUNG POET

SAVORING SPRING

A PHOTO ESSAY BY KATHRIN KOSCHITZKI

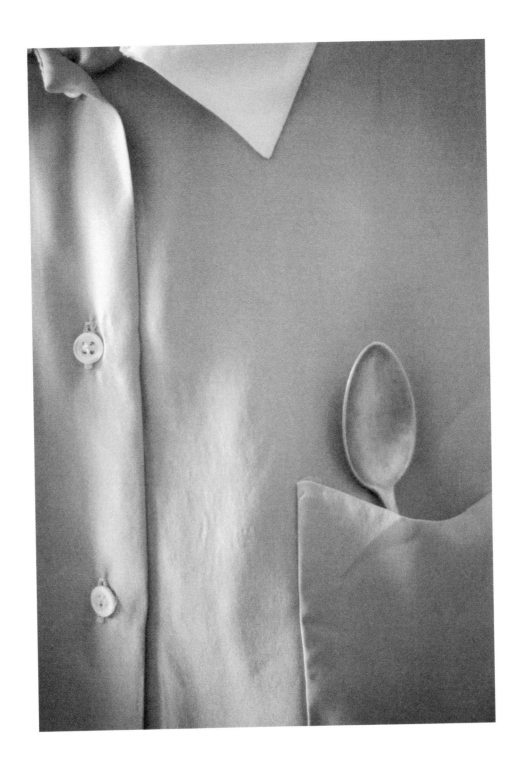

OLIVIA
TE CUIDA
SANTA TERESA 8
28004 MADRID
WWW.OLIVIATECUIDA.COM

OLIVIA TE CUIDA

A crate of oranges sits outside the kitchen while inside,
Marian prepares dishes using family recipes and locally grown produce.

Graced with a vase holding a sprig of hyacinth, the table by the French window is what I always hope for when I arrive for a meal at Olivia Te Cuida. If the weather is good, the window will be open and I'll get to watch Madrileños stroll by Calle Santa Teresa while I sip my *café con leche*. It is a small and simple joy, as is everything about Olivia Te Cuida.

Spanish for "Olivia takes care of you," Olivia Te Cuida opened in February 2009 as an oasis for those seeking peace and quiet in the Spanish capital—not to mention healthy, affordable food. "We wanted to take care of the working person," explained Esther Campoy, who runs the four-table restaurant with her husband, Fernando Fuentes, and her sister, Marian. While most Spanish restaurants close their kitchens around 2 p.m. and reopen for dinner, Olivia Te Cuida is open from 9 a.m. to 6 p.m. and is closed on weekends, proving that it's more than just a restaurant; it's a lifestyle.

The Campoy sisters share a meticulous eye for detail; they drew from their backgrounds in art and design when creating the restaurant's menu and interior. "It is a reflection of our taste," says Marian, a photographer-turned-cook. "We wanted it to feel like a second home." With raw oak floors and bare, eggshell-colored walls, Olivia Te Cuida manages to be aesthetically minimal and cozy. Strangers commune together at the large, stainless steel table in the center of the room, where toasters are readily at hand. A crate of oranges sits outside the kitchen while inside, Marian prepares dishes using family recipes and locally grown produce. "We use the same recipes we use in our kitchens at home," says Marian. "It's wholesome cooking but nothing too sophisticated."

The menu is divided into salads, vegetables, and grains, and includes dishes like mint couscous—with chickpeas and sun-dried tomatoes—and roasted aubergine topped with pomegranate seeds, scamorza cheese, and pine kernels. The chocolate tart with sprinkled saffron is a popular pick amongst the desserts.

Initially nervous about their limited space, the Campoy sisters are happy with their choice and determined to keep Olivia Te Cuida small and in the family. They even asked two close friends to join the team as waiters. There is hardly a lull during business hours, and reservations are highly recommended to get a table. "Because it's so small, it was full from the very beginning," says Marian, laughing.

WORDS BY STEPHANIE CORRAL
PHOTOGRAPHS BY JESSICA COMINGORE

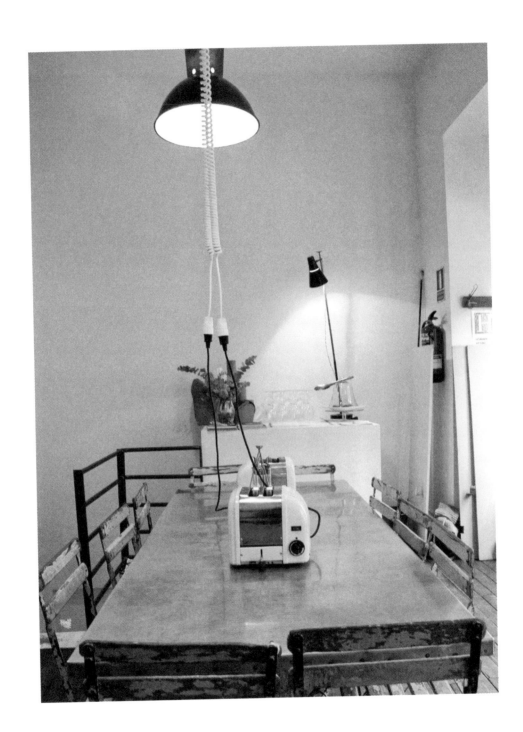

THE GOODNESS OF HANDCRAFTED GIFTS

The best decorating tip my wife and I ever received was from a friend who told us the secret of making a new residence feel like home: incorporate something handcrafted by someone we know into each room.

A quilt made by your grandmother is more heartwarming than one with questionable stains found in a thrift store—and decidedly more sanitary. No expensive china can rival a handmade mug, and cocoa somehow tastes sweeter when its vessel was made with care and love. Nails sink into drywall with more joy when you hang a piece of art created by your spouse rather than a print purchased from IKEA. The human touch of these handmade objects reaches out and grabs you right in the chest.

I am very fond of making and giving gifts. I'm not sure of the origin of this impulse; perhaps it came from every parent's unending delight in receiving crayon-scrawled drawings on cardboard. Maybe it came from something deeper and darker from my subconscious, an unconscious demand for acceptance by the recipient. I'm sure a therapist could hash it all out and tell me exactly why I like giving away my handmade items, but for me I'm pretty certain it has something to do with crocheting.

I love to crochet, though I don't fit the stereotype of the eighty-year-old grandmother (she could probably crochet me under the table). The crochet needles are spiritual for me, something akin to fingering prayer beads, and the repetition of movement puts me into a trance-like state.

If I didn't give away the things I crocheted, I would soon have cozies around everything—afghans filling the cupboards, scarves around every neck, hats on every head, iPods triple covered, and hot pads falling out of every kitchen drawer. "The greatest gift is a portion of thyself," said Ralph Waldo Emerson. But I'm pretty sure he meant, "The greatest gift is a crocheted scarf, if for no other reason than to save your home from crochet clutter."

The best decorating tip my wife and I ever received was from a friend who told us the secret of making a new residence feel like home: incorporate something handcrafted by someone we know into each room. We didn't have the luxury of home ownership or a long lease to get comfortable in our first apartment. Instead, we decorated with paintings done by friends, crocheted hot pads from our neighbors, quilts from our grandmothers, and photographs and art we each had created—items that could and would follow us and became the real indicators of our home. These physical objects contained pieces of our history and genealogy, pieces of our inspiration and aesthetic sense, and they fit together in the rooms to form the completed puzzle of our new life together. Handcrafted items transformed a two-bedroom, one-bath, six-month-lease apartment into our home.

All art creation is therapeutic for the creator, but should we subject others to our therapeutic manifestations? I may imagine I have woven a piece of myself into each item I have crocheted, but what are you really going to do with a red beanie for a Kewpie doll? For every moment of enchanted magic created by a handcrafted gift, there is the equal potential for unwanted voodoo.

As my crocheting fetish shows, the mere making of a handcrafted gift (absent the maternal gush) is not going to be sufficient to transform an apartment into a home. The goodness of the handcrafted gift comes not just from the skill of the crafter, but the crafter's empathetic resonance with the recipient and the recipient's need to possess and display a part of someone else. And what is more human and more good than that?

PHOTOGRAPH BY ALPHA SMOOT AND STYLING BY ANNE SMOOT

WORDS BY DAVID WINWARD

THE COOK'S ATELIER

Inspired by the traditions and culture of Burgundy, one American is living her dream and has created The Cook's Atelier in Beaune, France.

There are people in life that are compelled to leave both the place where they were born and the culture in which they were raised, all in the name of love. That's what I did, but it wasn't for a man. I moved to Beaune, France, for the love of good food, family traditions, and the pursuit of something special: a life rich in simplicity, the French markets, and a culture passionate about its culinary traditions.

Tucked away on a tiny street in the historic center of Beaune is The Cook's Atelier, a small cooking school devoted to exploring the regional culinary traditions, local food artisans, and the small family farms in Burgundy. Beaune is a well-preserved medieval city in the center of the Côte d'Or winemaking region. It's the perfect small French town with quaint cafes, wonderful *patisseries*, and *boulangeries* that still bake bread from scratch. It's an international town with a quiet, fierce, Burgundian pride, rooted in traditions.

For a cook, Burgundy is heaven on earth. Having left the restaurant business, I traveled to France to immerse myself in the culture and was given the opportunity to work with noted teacher and cookbook author, Anne Willan, at her chateau in Burgundy. It was such a life-changing experience for me that I flew back to the States, sold everything, and moved to France full-time to pursue my dream. I imagined a special place where people could learn to cook, a business that supported the local artisan food producers and sustainable agriculture; I have been passionate about the connection between the farmer and the cook since long before it was popular. Most importantly, I wanted to create a *lieu de convivialité*—a place where people come together, cook, and have a good time.

As you open the door to The Cook's Atelier, you quickly realize you are in for a special treat. Guests are welcomed by aromas from the kitchen and are greeted with a glass of chilled *crémant*, the region's sparkling wine. The table is set with fresh flowers, and plenty of candlelight fills the room. Fine glassware mixes with vintage French linen napkins, and an assortment of winter squash adorns the fireplace. The apartment is a light-filled space and the décor is simple, with wooden floors and pale walls. The season's offerings are casually displayed on creamy white vintage French platters, and they fill the apartment with the colors of the season. There's a large bowl filled with apples just picked from the garden, and Madame Petit's cornichons are displayed on the dining room buffet. Open shelves, lining the walls in the *atelier*, are filled with vintage finds from the local *brocantes*, homemade *confiture*, and favorite cookbooks. Vegetables gathered from the morning's visit to Madame Loichet's garden fill the table in the kitchen.

The Cook's Atelier is a magical place where people come together to celebrate real food, made from scratch. No chef's whites here; it's real cooking in the tradition of French grandmothers rather than *haute cuisine*. The Cook's Atelier is much more than a traditional cooking school; the convivial aspects and the friendships that are formed are just as important as the recipes. You never know with whom you will be sharing dinner —guests come from all over the world to cook and share a meal together. We honor the relationships that we have with the people who spend their lives growing good food, as well as the traditions passed down from generations of cooks. We work with locals such as Monsieur Méneger, a chef and farmer who is passionate about heritage breeds of pigs and chickens; Madame Loichet, who gathers the produce from her garden for the Saturday morning market in Beaune; Monsieur Vossot, an artisan butcher who takes pride in preserving the craft of the traditional French butcher; Madame Petit, who always has fresh eggs; and Madame Pechoux, who grows the most beautiful winter greens I have ever seen. It's more than just a cooking class; it's a unique experience that fosters the connection between the farmer and the cook. Lifelong friendships are made among the guests as they share a meal and a good glass of Pinot Noir. They learn the techniques of traditional French food in a relaxing and convivial environment, and they learn the importance of connecting with the people who grow the food that they eat.

Good food is so much more than recipes; it's about sharing a meal with those you love, learning new traditions, and creating traditions of your own. So pour yourself a glass of wine, and prepare a special dinner for your family and friends in celebration of simple food and good company around the table.

PHOTOGRAPH BY YOUNG & HUNGRY

WORDS BY MARJORIE TAYLOR

LUNCH IN FRANCE

I found myself sitting up a little straighter, arranging my dishes neatly in front of me,
putting my fork down between bites, truly tasting.

The twinkling lights outlining the terrace were what drew me in, despite the brightness of the midday sun. Some days I would spend hours walking around Bordeaux trying to pick out a place to eat lunch. I was equally infatuated with every café, and I ended up making the decision based on silly things—the color of the awnings, which chairs looked perfectly woven, if the people eating there looked French, if the word "truffle" was on the menu. But on this particular day, I fell for the twinkling lights.

It didn't take long for me to realize that lunch in France is not something to be taken lightly. For those couple of hours during the middle of the day, shops close, children go home from school, and town centers are virtually abandoned in order to honor this meal that's so carefully considered, it feels more like a sacred ritual. It is the main meal of the day; there's always wine, there's always dessert, and it always lasts for hours. This is not to say the food itself is extravagant—*niçoise* salad, mussels and fries, a basic *croque-monsieur*; the allure of lunch in France is the effortless elegance with which it is achieved.

Sitting under those twinkling lights, I became acutely aware of my surroundings. I found myself sitting up a little straighter, arranging my dishes neatly in front of me, putting my fork down between bites, truly *tasting*. I couldn't help noticing the gray-haired couple with matching striped shirts next to me, quietly giggling over a bottle of rosé. Priorities are just different in France, and it shows.

Lunch in France is special. It's the kind of experience that, when undertaken, should be one's sole and primary focus. It's about using straightforward ingredients to create meaningful meals. It's about enjoying the people around you or embracing the time alone. It's about slowing down and appreciating the unsuspecting moments.

We can't all have lunch in France every day, but it doesn't matter. A carafe of wine, a fresh-baked *baguette*, and simple linens are all easily attained elements; it's the thoughtful perspective that's worthy of admiration. Lunch in France is about acknowledging the little things that make life beautiful, and always leaving time for a post-lunch *sieste*.

PHOTOGRAPHS BY KATHRIN KOSCHITZKI AND LAURA DART
WORDS BY OLIVIA RAE JAMES

TWO

ENTERTAINING FOR TWO

∘ ∘

REVISITING OUR TEMPLES

*We came together at the tables of the most ordinary places,
which would soon become sacred.*

We started with lunch. I met him on a soggy, chilled afternoon in March. Across the table, he fidgeted with the zipper on his sweater. We were almost alone in a restaurant with an enveloping atmosphere and dark curtains serving as doors. I tried my first plate of Jewish fare. We ordered latkes and blintzes—hot little delicious things, golden from cooking and ready for dipping in sauce and cream. We talked and laughed and were nervous together, but this is how it starts, is it not? We strung together facts over the noise of forks on plates, cups on tables, and chairs on floors. We peeled back the layers of favorites: books, movies, and music. Our lunch date was a brief hour but it was dense, crowded with our identities, the facts of our lives, and a mutual understanding that we were more than happy to give each other that hour.

My now-husband and I got together during one of the most chaotic stages in each of our lives. I juggled my final year of university and a part-time job; he had several different jobs of his own. Free time was a luxury, but our crazy schedules somehow allowed us a period of true courtship. We got to know each other carefully, over good meals on frigid days and long walks home through the snow. The mess of everyday life faded quickly when we were together, one hour here, another there. We stole every moment we could get, and in those moments, while we were still living very separate lives, we came together at the tables of the most ordinary places, which would soon become sacred. They became our romantic touchstones. Those places, with their soon-to-be familiar menus, became historical settings for two people who did not yet have a history.

We've kept that date every year since. Meeting for lunch at that café, we order the same items we did the first time around, and the weather is always cool and testy with shades of gray bouncing all over the sky. The shyness has faded between us and the conversation is now all about our life. Stories are no longer new, but sitting to tell them is still important. Our lunch date has become a ritual for the two of us; it is a sweet and simple occasion that prompts us to notice how far we have come as a pair, a reminder that once we were strangers and now we are partners. There are so many memories in between those dates, moments that can dissolve if we are not careful to hold onto them.

So we punctuate our relationship with these ceremonial feasts. They are a way for us to reflect, looking back at everything finished, and a way for us to look forward, keeping our momentum going along with our changing life. Across the table, the giddiness of newness is no longer there, but is replaced by the excitement of our plans for the future. Sometimes it feels as though there is a huge distance separating us from the two bodies that got together years ago. We are not the same people who spent hours smiling over coffee on worn-out sofas at the place that was right between where I worked and he lived. I would order mine black, making a point that his was too light for me, and promptly forget about the coffee—I was in it for his eyes. Years later, we share a home and do not need to go anywhere to buy time together; I steal sips of his coffee, and I am now used to the taste of cream and sugar.

At home, we bring out white tapered candles for special dinners, and we enjoy the low, warm light and play Nat King Cole in the background. In the glow, the sound, the mundane day's thieves go away. There is no more complaining about work or about the weather; it stops being an ordinary day and turns into quite the night, resplendent with a quiet romance and a real sense of knowing that this is where we belong. We enter a divine state where only the two of us exist; we are absorbed in the moment of being together, and we slow down and pay attention. We consume each other's presence, talking quietly and laughing honestly. These moments feel sacred to us, and are and reminiscent of our second date, where the symphony of a failed curry dinner faded into the background. He grabbed my hand and we danced right there in his tiny living room.

On these quiet evenings, there may even be some singing, if he pulls out his guitar and if I have had enough to drink. I am not a singer, but with this man, in the candlelight, I can be braver than I am accustomed to. At our little meals, we are stable in what we mean to each other, even if we are now anxious to build a family, eager for the promise of large family dinners and lots noise all over the house. It is in those precise moments, at our own little temples, that we try to calm down and be aware of each other—because what do you have if you do not pay homage? Where do you go if you do not remember? We have our dates, our history, and our love. We take care of those things because they are who we are.

WORDS BY M.F. MILLER

PHOTOGRAPHS BY CELINE KIM

AUSTIN & DESMOND

---

*The bond that is created brings value and meaning to our lives
in an unexplainable, innate way.*

Maintaining a connection with nature is integral for balance in our lives, and few relationships are as available and helpful to our well-being as the relationship between humans and animals. The bond that is created brings value and meaning to our lives in an unexplainable, innate way.

Although there is debate over whether or not a dog is really "man's best friend," the significance of a relationship between man and dog cannot be denied. Selflessness, loyalty, devotedness, unconditional love—qualities that are commonly found in companionship with a dog—are not often found elsewhere. Something special exists in this space. A comfort, a constant. A friend.

STYLING AND WORDS BY ELISE YETTON
PHOTOGRAPH BY AUSTIN GROS

TWO WEEK EXPERIMENT

WORDS BY PAUL AND BRITTANY JEPSEN

PHOTOGRAPHS BY HILDA GRAHNAT

Breakfasts shared with co-workers before early-morning meetings can easily lapse into awkward silence. But when you have awoken your spouse an hour early to eat breakfast and spend morning time together, quiet easily envelops you both with a calm sort of togetherness. Conversation sputters, but it has the same soothing effect as lying in bed as a child listening to your dad trying to start the car on a frosty winter morning. It feels regular and familiar, but important at the same time.

Naturally, we each have stories of past mornings. We would wake up in a certain way or be woken by a particular person or sound. We would eat something, be it a bowl of oatmeal or a random combination of food the fridge had to offer. But behind the details and routines, what were the human connections?

In our search to find stimulating morning rituals we looked comparatively at family examples of the past. Almost immediately we thought of Brittany's grandparents and realized that our mornings were mere blank pages compared to their daily prologue.

Carl and Dorothy Bradshaw had a knack for the natural. Overnighting grandchildren knew not to expect Cap'n Crunch in the morning, but homemade bran muffins or whole wheat toast with lettuce and peanut butter—the kind with the oil on top. Dinner would likewise be healthy, often with yams for dessert, hold the brown sugar and marshmallows, thank you very much.

Mind you, this was Bel Air in West Los Angeles—the West Los Angeles before it was "West LA" and before quaint Bel Air became overgrown with larger-than-life faux Tuscan villas. When Brittany's mom and her siblings were growing up, they raised goats in their backyard and drank their raw milk. They would gather fresh eggs from the trees that their Bantam chickens had somehow climbed. They called guinea pigs, rabbits, and pretty much anything that entered their yard their pets and allowed them to run freely. It was a free-range paradise.

Any relative or friend of the Bradshaws would describe them as peaceful, humble, and kind. They weren't the type to talk much; perhaps it was an effect of Carl growing up on a wheat farm or Dorothy's naturally calm demeanor. Their love was like their food, wholesome and homegrown, and perhaps that's why their house was a constant venue for out-of-town guests, gatherings, baby showers, and wedding receptions. They loved the sociality of friends and family in one place.

In homage to Carl and Dorothy, we decided it was time for an experiment. We would attempt to eat breakfast together every day for two weeks, a ritual we had not performed in quite some time. At the same time we tried to inject the germ of Bradshaw culture into the Petri dish of our living room. No chickens flocked around our Copenhagen apartment and goats did not graze in between our bookshelves, but we did eat whole grains and seek out the wholesome.

We wound our electric alarm clocks ahead to 6 a.m., giving ourselves a half hour of breakfast time. The first day started like the first day of a diet—optimistic and full of gusto. By this time in the yearly calendar the Danish winter had arrived, dictating an 8:30 a.m. sunrise, but we weren't fazed by the darkness. We embraced it by lighting candles, as all good Danes do. Carl and Dorothy were on our minds as we ate a simple meal of oats and chatted more about their rituals.

In the memories of their children, Carl often told Dorothy to stay in bed while he prepared a well-balanced breakfast and then chauffeured them off to early-morning dance rehearsals and school. Our meals, on the other hand, were only a rudimentary emulation of theirs, with store-bought clementines and the occasional home-baked loaf.

As with most diets and resolutions, our enthusiasm waned over the two weeks. Oftentimes, we found ourselves succumbing to dazed sleepiness and then compensating by chomping on leftovers as we got ready. But overall, we came to cherish our morning time. It became a space to talk about plans for the day, remember stories of our own childhoods, and laugh over odd fragments of dreams. It became whole-grain nourishment both to the body and the soul. By mimicking the lifestyle patterns of those beloved grandparents, we were able to tap into a sometimes-forgotten way of life. We gained a higher respect for Carl and Dorothy's generation, where time didn't seem to press as hard—or was it just more normal to prioritize family time back then? The germ of their precious morning pastimes had a hard time surviving in the hostile environment of our modern life, but a little shoot from the past survived. ○

MAX AND ME

Joy can be measured by the amount of ingredients on the floor,
happiness by sugar glittered across the forehead.

We meet in a still and quiet morning kitchen, just as the sun begins to dart across the room and burn into the countertops. Sleepy little eyes and chilly hands warm up over an open oven door. Woolens shuffle on wooden floors while mixing bowls clink and chime with the clock. I grab the flour and sugar; he tends to the eggs and butter. Such is our tradition. A mother and her son, armed only with a stained recipe card passed down a generation and the knowledge that we just might be the only two souls awake in all the wide world.

These are the times when saying the most means using the fewest words. We communicate through a laugh, a taste from the bowl, through the rhythm of mixing and kneading soft dough or the tapping of a leveled-off cup of flour. The hush heightens the senses, making the metal bowls colder, the cinnamon and yeast the most exotic bouquet either of us have ever taken in. With every move I make I have a tiny shadow right behind me, grabbing at my hands with a sweet and funny eagerness to be a part of every last step. There is a profound sense of self for a little one in each move of the recipe card. Small absolutes to stand firm on, instructions for sweet rolls and for life—a cup of this and this, a pinch of that, stirred together, will result in something wonderful. Adding butter to anything takes it to the heavens. And sometimes, most times, half the fun is setting the card aside and winging it.

We sit and watch the dough rise; finding the sunniest part of the house, we sit like lazy cats stretched out across the floor. And we wait. It's during this time, somewhere between the rolls going into the oven and the stirring of the icing, that I get to hear the wildest tales of a boy and his day-to-day life—silly stories and tiny peeks into who this little person is and what makes him go 'round.

Together we create disasters and we create confectionary masterpieces. Just the two of us and our quiet morning kitchen. Making messes is just part of having passion, and we are nothing if not passionate. Joy can be measured by the amount of ingredients on the floor, happiness by sugar glittered across the forehead. I think about my mother and grandmothers, the way I would watch them dance across their kitchens with such confidence and ease. The only thing precious was our time together; everything else could be cleaned up, fixed, thrown out, or started over. And dishes could always, always wait. It's these truths that I have packed up and taken along with me as a woman and now as a mama. It's these truths I hope to instill in my little one with each toss of flour, each eggshell retrieved from the batter.

It's about being present, sharing, giving, tasting, learning, and being still enough to appreciate it all.

PHOTOGRAPH AND WORDS BY KATIE STRATTON

AN UNREMARKABLY CASUAL THING

It had started, years ago, with a lunch. Just one shared meal: an unremarkably casual thing.

At this moment, life is a whirlwind. Eight days from now I will marry the best friend I have ever known. She is a rare find and I am the luckiest of treasure hunters. It is a remarkably exciting time, brimming with anticipation and activity. But make no mistake—it is a whirlwind. We are spinning with every emotion: we are happy and sentimental, confident and nervous, focused and scattered, but mostly we are busy. Busy with preparations for the guests, the ceremony, the parties, the honeymoon, the lifetime we wake up to when the carnival dust settles. I suppose every couple that has put on a wedding will relate to this. And yet, as crazy as it all is, it's hard to get frustrated when working toward such a special moment. Like tired parents on Christmas Eve setting the stage for the magic of Christmas morning, we continue to work to make every detail glow. It is a lovely kind of storm we are in.

As I write this I am, frankly, overwhelmed by the wealth of things left on our still-to-do list. There are centerpieces to finish making, neckties to buy, programs to print, and twinkling lights to hang. Yet, as I consider all there is left to do before we close the dating chapter of our life and open the married one, I can't help but recall how our story first began—back before the bouquets and the giant cake and the first dance and the waiters with trays of champagne. Back before we were even friends. Long before the wind turned all around us.

It had started, years ago, with a lunch. Just one shared meal: an unremarkably casual thing.

"Just lunch?" she had asked with a raised eyebrow and faux suspicion. "Yeah, it could be fun. I know about this local farm that makes these incredible homemade sandwiches and muffins; I've been looking for an excuse to go out there," I replied. An excuse to go out there? An excuse to have lunch—really? But, then again, I suppose all first dates are a kind of pretense—an excuse to secure the undivided attention of another, scaffolding for potentially bigger things. Risky business. Small jumps from tall bluffs.

As we snaked along the narrow Ozark Mountain roads we talked comfortably, sharing a new level of confidence, careful not to betray any frailties of character, while also doing our best to be honest. I told her about Europe and she told me all about her dad. She wore a blue top over olive skin and she smiled as easily as she breathed. She was a newly discovered country, an unfolding brown-eyed mystery. An increasingly bright and playful spirit grew between us—we weren't ready to talk about it but we couldn't ignore it. So we ordered lunch. And then we ate very well: shiitake mushrooms grown in the dark of the farm's old barn, homemade fruit-infused barbecue sauce, the infamous blueberry "thunder muffin," fresh and warm and paired with homemade vanilla bean ice cream. It was hillbilly *joie de vivre*. We ate and talked and ate and laughed, the whole time watching blackbirds dive in and out of the dusty aisles of berry trees. We sat for hours. We talked to the farmer. We drank iced tea. We were in no kind of hurry.

At some point (maybe when the sky began leaning toward dusk), sitting there at a crooked

As a work in progress—friendship is never finished—our love is a shape shifter,
a garden for tending, a working title, a remarkably un-casual thing.

wooden picnic table, something changed. Lunch had become something else—a metamorphosis had occurred. Our simple shared meal, the unremarkably casual thing, had opened the door to a new idea—that the two of us could become friends. Perhaps even great friends. The kind of friends who could happily share many more long meals together, and share long hours of undivided attention, telling tall tales and daily truths. The kind of friends who find the many unremarkably casual things of life transfigured into deep moments of joy, simply because they are shared with one another.

Nothing was decided while driving away from the farm that June day; we made no specific commitments, no future plans, and we had no idea what would come next. We had shared a lunch and we couldn't have known, then, about the coming years of work that would be built into our friendship: the long-distance phone calls, the

plane tickets, the handmade gifts, the maturing of expectations, the surrendering of fears, the shared successes, and the forgiveness of failings. Work has been done, is being done, and will be done until we are parted by death. As a work in progress—friendship is never finished—our love is a shape shifter, a garden for tending, a working title, a remarkably un-casual thing.

I do not know what would have happened if we hadn't gone to the farm that first day or where our lives will go from here. Right now I can barely see past our still-to-do list and our much-anticipated honeymoon getaway. But I can clearly see where we first began to believe in the mystery of a forever kind of friendship: a golden summer day, two souls willing to give undivided attention, birds and berries and a belief in becoming something new. A great adventure story begun years ago with a lunch—the first in a lifetime of meals shared together.

PHOTOGRAPHS BY ALEC VANDERBOOM AND LAURA DART
WORDS BY AUSTIN SAILSBURY

FEW
ENTERTAINING FOR A FEW

○ ○ ○

CHICKEN AND EGG

PHOTOGRAPHS BY JEN ALTMAN

WORDS BY ASHLEY ENGLISH

As we gather eggs and collect vegetables, he bears firsthand witness to the circular nature of life. It's not a linear progression, the route from farm to table, from field to fork. It's elliptical, moving in ever-evolving, always-rotating circles.

M ost mornings—after changing the baby's diaper, putting on the coffee, and placating the chorus of four meowing cats—I put my young son into his carrier and head to the chicken coop. As the sun begins to crest the mountain ridge behind our home, we walk out the back door, down the hill, past the beehives, beside the vegetable garden, and pause at the coop gate. His interest is piqued by the gentle clucks calling from behind the henhouse door; he kicks his legs in anticipation and excitement. We unlock the latches, swing the door open widely, and greet the flock with calls of, "Hi chickies!" and, "Good morning, ladies!" Together we bend over to offer them fresh water and feed and, often, a treat of sorts like an apple core, a bit of cracked corn, or a handful of wild strawberries or wineberries picked from our yard *en route*.

Later in the day, after hearing raucous squawking heralding the arrival of an egg, we again journey to the coop. He and I gather up the hen's orbed offerings and express our gratitude, sometimes in the form of a pat on their silky plumage, other times by tossing an interloping bug or worm their way. We retreat to the house, gathering collard greens and herbs in the garden along the way. With his papa, we chop the greens and herbs, crack the eggs and beat them until golden, and add everything to a pan along with a generous dollop of butter. Together we cook a frittata from what we've grown and gathered.

I always knew I'd want my children to know where food came from. Now I realize that more than just knowing a fruit or vegetable or pork chop's provenance, my son is learning lessons in living. As we gather eggs and collect vegetables, he bears firsthand witness to the circular nature of life. It's not a linear progression, the route from farm to table, from field to fork. It's elliptical, moving in ever-evolving, always-rotating circles. He sees the food we feed our flock, or the seeds we sow in the garden produce food. He watches us cook that food. He looks on as we take the scraps left from the meal to the compost, or back to the flock, in turn producing more food. He sees growth and harvest and decay. He sees fellowship and community and camaraderie as we dine with friends, or simply as a small family, together. ○

SPOONING

In every new village or bustling city we settled into, I purchased a spoon. Or two.

About a month or so after we got married, my new husband and I embarked on a honeymoon that would forever change us. We didn't go to Hawaii or spend a couple weeks in Mexico; we began saving our pennies the moment we got serious, and after our marriage we set out to live in South India, Vietnam, and Turkey for a year. We wanted to see a bit of how the rest of the world lives and get to know ourselves in the process.

In every new village or bustling city we settled into, I purchased a spoon. Or two. In Hanoi, I asked a cafe owner if I might buy the neon orange and baby blue plastic spoons we'd swirled our sweetened iced coffees with; she looked perplexed and giggled (silly American lady!), but she threw in the tall, colorful utensils with our bill, refusing to accept the money I tried to stuff into her plaid apron pocket. A variation on this routine was repeated in multiple languages across the world.

I'm grateful I continued my happy treasure hunt. I had a hunch this precious collection would delight me with each swirl of my PG Tips and cream, every lick of peanut butter in between deadlines, and every surreptitious bite from a new tub of yogurt and honey while I gazed into the fridge contemplating dinner. Indeed, our worldly gallivants came to an end, and we are now settled into our own cozy palace in the clouds of Portland, Oregon. But I can't shake the sparkly feeling of touching the unknown while on the road with my ritual warm brews and little bites—and I don't want to. For a moment, I'm transported: we are ducking into a chai shack deep in the coconut groves, motorcycling along the highway with *bánh mì* sandwiches tucked into our pockets, and we are sipping black Turkish tea (sugar cubes clenched in our teeth) with the fishermen on Galata Bridge in Istanbul. And in those memories, with my sweet spoons, I am home.

WORDS AND PHOTOGRAPH BY LEELA ROSS

ON DEVOTION
A SMALL MONTRÉAL GATHERING

WORDS BY NATASHA PICKOWICZ

PHOTOGRAPHS BY JOHN CULLEN

About one year ago, I moved to Montréal to live with my partner, the writer Adam Leith Gollner. Though I was thrilled by our blossoming love, it took me much longer to initiate a romance with the city. Adam, who is a native Montréaler, did his best to welcome me into his life. And while I felt very close to him, I still felt like a foreigner. As a San Diego–born California girl, I discovered that I didn't know how to relate to Montréal's glamorous French Canadian inhabitants. It takes time to acclimatize to a new place, I knew, but Montréal—with its own distinct culture, language, and complicated history—was somehow different. If a city could be a person, then I was deeply intimidated by how cool and sophisticated she was.

I spent those first few months charting tentative steps around the borders of an impressive city. As way of navigating the impenetrable haze of my new world, I turned to cooking for comfort, grace, and answers. A cozy, down-to-earth neighborhood restaurant called Dépanneur Le Pick Up hired me to be their baker, and I worked long afternoons in their cramped kitchen, stirring scone dough and brownie batter until my forearms ached and my hair was dusted with flour. Afterward, I raced home on my bicycle, bags leaden with my leftover pastry, to make dinner with Adam.

Cooking meals with Adam—a man as blissfully starry-eyed with food as I—was like discovering paradise. I like to think that it is the moments that Adam and I pad around the kitchen together, stirring and slurping and laughing, when I feel most comfortable, most myself. So we entertained often, and our elaborate dinner parties became my way of letting Montréal know that I hadn't given up yet. As I shared my roast chicken, chocolate cake, and Kate Bush record collection at parties that leaned late into the night, I finally felt like I was starting to fit in.

Gradually, I began making my own contributions to the community, and casual acquaintances transformed into tight friendships. I volunteered at an experimental music festival called Cool Fest, and grew close to Katherine Kline, a meditative, serious musician studying psychoanalysis. I started organizing culinary workshops at Dépanneur Le Pick Up, and got to know Camilla Wynne, a cheerful pastry chef who founded an independent canning business called Preservation Society. I bonded with my neighbor Rebecca West, a native Montréaler who works in communications for the arts, over her mischievous kitten, Penelope. I hand-rolled trays of truffles for Himo Martin, the dashing, roguish artist behind the jewelry line Pearls and Swine, for his special events.

So when I heard from my beloved childhood friend James Henry, a psychiatric resident living in San Francisco, who wrote that he was planning to visit me in Montréal, I knew I had to throw him one of our glorious dinner parties. James and I became close at age twelve, at a moment when my adolescent admiration for him seemed nearly boundless. In the fifteen years since, we have been each other's dates at awkward winter dances, moshed our way through sweaty punk concerts, and hitchhiked our way around southern Spain. And even as we moved diagonally across the continent, like repelling magnets or boomerangs flung too far, we've grown, inexplicably, even tighter.

James has always viewed the kitchen as a playground, and with delight. For this, James's first ever trip to The Great White North, I imagined the ways our time together in Montréal could crystallize into the next chapter of our story. Before James arrived, Adam and I spent quite a few evenings swapping ideas for the feast. (The distinct joy of the dinner party is never limited to the moment of the meal.) First, I wrote to Katherine, Camilla, Himo, and Rebecca, already

fantasizing about how much everyone would love my old friend. Then, Adam and I researched dishes, read through books, tested recipes, and made multiple trips to the market. Discussing venues, we agreed that Himo's home, a cavernous loft in Old Montréal, would be a dreamy setting for our simple, French-influenced feast.

The morning of our dinner party, still bleary-eyed, we made a stop at Dépanneur Le Pick Up for *allongés* (the Montreal equivalent of an Americano) and bacon-tomato sandwiches before heading to Marché Jean-Talon, a sprawling outdoor market in Petite Italie. I picked out two splintering wooden crates packed with Malpeque oysters from Prince Edward Island, and we drove to Old Montreal, already longing for that first sip of Chablis.

As James and I began unloading groceries at Himo's apartment, guests started to arrive. Introductions were made, the first bottle of wine finally uncorked. Because I wanted James to experience our classically French style of cooking, the afternoon unfolded like a "Greatest Hits" of our home cooking repertoire. I like creating everything from scratch, often focusing on more idiosyncratic or old-fashioned recipes that I rarely see at the typical dinner table. As I put our friends to task washing lettuce and dicing shallots, I set out bowls of warm *gougères*, a savory, moist choux pastry made with shredded Gruyère. They were gobbled up in moments.

Earlier in the week, Adam requested my homemade *gravlax*, fat and firm from its lengthy cure in bourbon and dark brown sugar, which I had made for his birthday a year earlier. At Himo's home, we sliced the *gravlax* into jagged sheets of silk, and ate it draped over toasts made from Montréal bagels, topped with tangy homemade *crème fraîche* and a whisper of dill. And there was wine, and so much of it—six or seven bottles, all carefully handpicked by Adam, a self-confessed Burgundy obsessive.

After we finished our snacks, we climbed a rickety ladder to Himo's rooftop and began shucking oysters. Camilla and Rebecca took control, unveiling the briny, viscous specimens faster than we could eat them. Stamping our feet in the brisk air, we gulped down oysters drenched in lemon juice and mignonette. Camilla, grasping the wooden handle of her shucker, pumped her fist into the sky. "This is…spectacular. I feel so *alive*!" she shouted. Maybe her outburst was the prompted by the long pulls of Fourchaune or the life-affirming mineral rush of oysters, but I felt it too, that chemistry of the rooftop winds and mysterious food spinning its magic inside me.

As the sun dipped into the horizon, I unveiled a chilled *jambon persillé*—an old-fashioned terrine with shredded ham, raw garlic, and minced parsley suspended in a wine-rich aspic—that Adam had assembled the night before. We ate thick slices of terrine with smears of Dijon mustard, cornichons, white country bread, and a simple green salad, draped in a fuzzy walnut oil vinaigrette. It was almost laughably simple—really just what you would bring to a proper picnic—but as my eyes rested on the drained bottles and widening smiles across the table, it felt almost unquestionably rich.

Because I am a baker and there must be a cake at every dinner party, I brought out a Provençal-style walnut gateau, sable-colored and with a coarse crumb and an unforgettable taste. It is a cake I never would have made prior to my exposure to French-Canadian culture, and I consider it a modest marker of my own growth in this city. As I cut the cake into slivers, I thought about those early, lean Montréal days, bereft of the golden warmth of the company I have now. I made a toast to James, my companion since the very beginning, my friend to whom I will be eternally devoted. "Thank you for coming to our city," I said. It slipped out. *Our* city. I didn't even know I had said it. But even as I uttered those words, I knew them to be true. My romance with the city had finally bloomed. ○

PREPARATIONS

A WORK OF FICTION

You've lived the in the city for a year and have decided it's time to host a party. Nothing showy, just a small gathering of your new friends and a modest array of *hors d'oeuvres* you've cobbled together from a wayward assortment of farmers' market fare. Soft cheese melts into crostini. Dried figs give easily under the weight of your knife.

As you put the finishing touches on the spread, a memory from your childhood takes shape. A visit from a great-aunt whose name you no longer remember, but whose scent of old roses and talcum powder still sits dormant in the back of your brain. She came on a weekday, which made the visit odd for you. Visitors were normally a thing saved for weekends, a drawn-out affair that spanned a meal or two. But there she was, carting her breathing machine through your living room as you softly cursed math problems with newly learned words on a spot of floor where the sunlight always pooled. She sat down in the armchair next to you without a word until she noticed your calves, dappled with fresh imprints from the knotty carpet. She leaned in and poked.

"Would you just look at that," she wheezed.

"Just look at that. Look at the muscles on you." She laughed and pinched your calf harder than you thought she could. To mask your bewilderment, you joined in her laughter. Your mother walked into the room at the sound of her laughter, and she spoke again, "Have you seen her legs? Those calves? This one will be just fine. Don't worry about her one bit." She turned to you. "Calves, my dear, they're the site of vitality on a woman, you know. Take proper care to let people know you're alive every once and a while." She patted your leg and winked.

Filtered through time, the fear and confusion informing this event have died away; its once-hard charcoaled lines have given way to ghostly outlines—a simple reminder from a woman who knew where you'd come from. Your friends will be here any minute, but you dash to your closet and pick out a cream skirt with delicate lace inlay. You slip off your jeans and twist out of your thick wool socks, nearly falling as you do. There's a knock at the door just as you clasp the skirt onto your waist. You take a breath and walk out of your bedroom, ready now.

ILLUSTRATION BY KATIE STRATTON

WORDS BY ANNIE BILANCINI

MORNING RITUALS

PHOTOGRAPHS BY BRITT CHUDLEIGH

WORDS BY CHRISTINA ROSALIE

There is something about these mornings that I can't describe. The way making breakfast with the kids is at once completely serene and totally helter-skelter.

Mornings start early with small children. There is no sleeping in, no gradual wakening. Instead there is the immediate, vivacious insistence of elbows and laughter. Little boys want to get up when the day is new and the sky is still pale like a bowl of milk. They clamber into bed with us, find nooks that are warm, burrow down for a minute or two, and then begin to chatter, giggle, tickle, poke. It isn't long before they claim that they are starving. The dog needs to be let out. Someone has jabbed a finger into someone else's eye. And so the days begin at our house: with hot showers, an urgent need for coffee, and then all of us around the butcher-block counter eating eggs.

I've found I need my morning coffee with a bit of sweetness and fortitude to make up for the inevitable sleep deficit I always owe, and there is nothing quite like the combination of frothed whole milk, a good double espresso, and a drizzle of dark maple syrup. The syrup is a Vermont tradition I've grown rather fond of. It suits our rural life—we live at the end of a dirt road on a hill among maples. In the woods you can still find old stone walls and every spring, just as the road turns to mud, our neighbors begin tapping trees and collecting sap. When we walk over to visit, hours slip by standing around the open evaporator, all of us enveloped in clouds of sweet steam. We return carrying mason jars of new golden syrup.

Rural living and small children define our morning rituals: getting up early, preparing coffee, and then heading out to the coop to bring back smooth oval eggs, still warm, tucked into pockets. Some mornings snow is falling; other days it rains, and mud fills the potholes in the roads. Sometimes there are crows calling from the bare branches of the poplars; other times we can hear cardinals calling territorially back and forth across the fields as we walk to the coop to feed the hens cracked corn and break ice from the water feeder.

It took me a long time to understand the many virtues of eggs for breakfast. In fact, I wasn't a breakfast person at all. But like good coffee, I've found that breakfast with a little heft to it has a way of fortifying a person after a night of not enough sleep. And fresh eggs fried with butter and a little thyme are simply magic if you toss a few slices of peasant bread into the pan with them, and let the butter make the edges of the toast all crispy and golden. This has become our breakfast ritual most week days: whatever hearty bread we bake or buy, fried alongside eggs, served sandwich style with

just a little jam, and then enjoyed together, all of us side by side, with more coffee or frothed milk for the kids. Then we're all leaving, pulling on jackets, trying to remember everything.

On the weekend there is more time. And because the pace is slower, we make a bigger deal out of breakfast: fluffy biscuits the boys help to cut out, served with butter and marmalade, bacon, and fried eggs. Or baked eggs, served in plain white ramekins, made with butter, scallions, cheddar, and thyme. The kids scorned these eggs—until they tried them, then asked for seconds. And most recently it's been a light, heavenly Dutch baby that's captured our love on the weekend. So airy it billows like a cloud from the cast iron pan before sinking back down on the plate to be served with fresh lemon juice, powdered sugar, and bacon.

There is something about these mornings that I can't describe. The way making breakfast with the kids is at once completely serene and totally helter-skelter. Invariably something gets spilled by the little one. He's three, and he wants very much to be involved in everything, pulling up a tall stool we keep around the butcher block island so that he can watch and stick his chubby fingers into whatever he can reach. The older one, who is seven, has grown up in the kitchen. He can pull a shot of espresso now, with crema thick on the top, and takes this job seriously: grinding, tamping, and pulling, while one of us helps the little one navigate the whisk around the big metal bowl, and the other melts butter in the cast iron skillet on the stove.

When we're baking, we fry bacon and then sip coffee while flipping through magazines or the newspaper, and have the perfect kind of small talk: inconsequential, full of little jokes and tidbits of news gleaned from the week. When the timer rings, the boys clatter to their spots at the table. The little one sits not in a high chair, but on the thickest unabridged Oxford dictionary, sometimes with his feet tucked up under him, now eager with his fork already in hand. Candles in jelly jars make the light soft; yellow cloth napkins are set at every place for sticky hands.

It's not something we ever planned, this ritual of mornings, of showing up early, and eating together to start the day. But it's the thing that sets everything on course for us for the rest of the day, and gives us this: a brief and pleasant ellipsis of gratitude. ○

JARS OF SUNSHINE

Summer seems transient in contrast with the cold days of winter,
and we wish for the sun's warm rays long before summer greets us again.

The intense Canadian winter can be daunting; by October, the hot and hazy days of summer are already a distant memory. Summer seems transient in contrast with the cold days of winter, and we wish for the sun's warm rays long before summer greets us again.

One of the things I miss most during the winter is being able to bite into fresh fruit, straight off the tree or snatched from a local farm basket. Peach season is fleeting, but remains one of my favorite highlights of mid-to-late August. Canning peaches in late summer is a strong Canadian tradition, designed to turn back the calendar during a deep winter siege.

My future husband's family has a 223-year-old fruit farm at the foot of the Niagara Escarpment, home to some of the best soil in North America, and they can peaches every year. A visit to Two Century Farm is exactly what I imagine time travel to be like. Things ebb and flow according to nature's schedule, just as they have for the past two centuries.

I treasure the stories I've heard of the Two Century Farm kitchen in full swing. The grandchildren remember it as "a big operation," Gran in the kitchen listening to the CBC or classical radio, surrounded by mountains of ripe peaches, strange-looking tools (like jar-lifting tongs, a lid lifter, a bubble freer, and a canning funnel), and witch-like cauldrons of boiling water. It was a time to give Gran her space, and more importantly, a time to stay out of the way. Hearing words like sterilization, pressure, bubbles, and seals, made the kitchen seem like a science laboratory to her grandchildren.

A winter's supply of canned peaches was stored in the musty, dark basement of the old farmhouse, and it was a precarious descent down the rickety steps to retrieve one of these precious jars. The grandchildren feared the darkness, but knew that being asked to fetch a peach jar was a real treat, glad that they were not being asked to find the less-exciting beets and gherkins stored in the same cellar.

After participating in the peach canning for the first time last summer, I asked how best to eat them. Turns out, you can consume the sun-drenched warmth of the peach orchards in a myriad of simple but delicious ways—tasty bites of sunshine to chase away the chill of even the worst Canadian winter.

WORDS AND PHOTOGRAPHS BY TRISH PAPADAKOS

TABLE DECONSTRUCTION

A PHOTO ESSAY BY LEO PATRONE

STYLING BY SARAH WINWARD

START

FINISH

My doctor told me to stop having intimate dinners for four.
Unless there are three other people.

ORSON WELLES 1915-1985

MARLOW & SONS

A GOOD PLACE TO GATHER

INTERVIEWS AND INTRO BY SAER RICHARDS
PHOTOGRAPHS BY SETH SMOOT
STYLING BY KENDRA SMOOT

THE ESTABLISHMENT

Marlow & Sons (a restaurant, café and store in Williamsburg, Brooklyn) is part of a Brooklyn restaurant group that includes Diner (a restaurant housed in an old Pullman car), Marlow & Daughters (a traditional butchery and general provisions store), and Romans (a Fort Greene, Brooklyn restaurant with a seasonal Italian-inspired menu).

When you enter the Marlow & Sons, it's hard to identify what exactly makes it so enticing and warm. Maybe it's the glow that emanates from nowhere specifically, but which still manages to bathe the whole place in light as though from a flickering fireplace. The furnishings have the wear and patina that tell many a story. Dark wood walls and a butcher-shop-style floor (sans wood shavings) provide the framework that houses gently worn tables made of robust wood with marble tops. Some are communal and others so intimate you can't help being drawn to the person sharing your space. The wall-long wooden bar is like an antiquated retaining wall, holding back rows upon rows of beverages from small-batch distilleries and a few bottles saved from a fire in the owner's uncle's warehouse.

The walls are punctuated with framed black-and-white pictures of people you think you might know and shelves of trophies you thought you saw won. These decorative elements are akin to those you would find in the home of an old, dear friend, not in a restaurant in Brooklyn—mere spitting distance from one of the most bustling, frenetic cities in the world. It feels as though time slows down in Marlow & Sons. Hunched shoulders relax. Conversation flows.

Aside from its congenial surroundings, there are other reasons that Marlow & Sons isn't your typical place to dine. An attached café and store teem with brands and objects that invoke curiosity. Locally made favorites abound, such as Mast Brothers Chocolate, Common Good cleaning products, and jjr aprons. Leather bags are made from the hides of the animals that are served in the restaurant and sold in the local butcher shop under the brand name Breton. Foreign staples like APC jeans, Fer à Cheval soaps, and Bodum coffee supplies are offered, as are items by other brands—such as Weleda—that have an enduring, holistic history. The mix is eclectic yet cohesive. It's not just goods that you want, but things you will eventually need, thoughtfully chosen for their origin, purpose, and story.

However, this unique yet effective combination of a restaurant, store, and café is not the extent of the Marlow & Sons appeal. Everyone at the establishment has a close relationship with the regional farmers who provide the produce and meats that are served on a daily basis. Quarterly, the entire staff travels to visit and help these farmland suppliers. Together they plant the greens for winter in the greenhouses and visit the cows and sheep that will soon pay the heftiest of sacrifices, traveling from farm to table. Marlow & Sons participates in the thoughtful animal program, purchasing a whole animal and using it in its entirety, and provides fresh cut meats to the public through the butchery.

This close proximity between one's food supplier and one's plate certainly fortifies an appreciation for all that is involved in creating a good dish. It is especially endearing to find that all those involved in the process are passionate about good food, sitting down to eat, and respecting the origins of one's goods—things that were the norm in yesteryear and today, are sadly found less often.

Marlow & Sons is not only a local restaurant; it is a local dining room, for it truly feels like an extension of one's own home. Eating here is like inviting a few close friends around for a bite, a feeling that is encouraged by the small yet ever-changing menu, featuring items more extraordinary than many cook in their own home, with fresh ingredients picked at their peak, and meats reared for two or more years with the express purpose of being in a delicious dish at the restaurant.

I wanted you to experience the same easy relationship that customers have with those who work at Marlow & Sons, so I talked to many of the people who make the restaurant what it is.

THE OWNERS

Andrew Tarlow and Kate Huling, the owners of Marlow & Sons, have had restaurant careers that have spanned their entire relationship. Marlow & Sons, Diner, Marlow & Daughters, and Romans are but an extension of their family.

There is an unmistakable glow that comes from Kate when she talks about the work they do. A glow that comes from a conviction for doing something she wholeheartedly believes in, and also from carrying the couples' fourth child. Andrew, on the other hand, is more subdued in demeanor but equally resolute. Their vision is united, and they are always looking for ways to be more thorough and careful in using the materials they purchase and provide to the community.

ANDREW TARLOW

Why is what you do so important?

In my mind, it's how we feel human. You are eating something that is made by hand, is fairly nutritious, and well thought out. We know the communication from that plate of food, to the producers, and have gone to visit them. To close the loop is to find the person who will eat it.

It's not usual to see a restaurant, café, and store in one. How did you decide that would work for you?

We didn't decide! That's not how we work. The original notion was, I hedged my bets. We had a busy restaurant next door, this space became available, and I didn't want anyone else to take it and I didn't believe we could fill another restaurant nor make enough with a store so we bisected it and worked hard at making it work. We have been very flexible with what we sell and how we sell it. It's been a real journey.

So it was more of an organic development?

Even the shape of that room has been redone three times. It operates half as a store and half as a café, and the café is busy now, has become another driving force of this business. In essence it would be equally good if it was just for coffee and we could own that skill set one hundred percent and move the store.

How would you describe your aesthetic?

I don't know if I have a defining word for it; it's definitely organic. I want things to feel handmade. A sense that someone made, say, this table. But we aren't veering off into places that feel like a look back in time to "then" without being curated. This room was a lot darker but everything here was made to wear down. We have replaced one table that wore down too far but we start with things that get better with age.

KATE HULING

Is it important for there to be a story behind your products?

I think it's more about the wholesomeness of it all. We used to live in a community where you had sheep and I had cows and our friends had chickens and we used to share and I would share the wool with you. I think that's one of the most meaningful of human interactions, helping each other live our lives. We can't do it all. We do it together. We have lost that sense. Now you go to the supermarket and see eggs in Styrofoam and you've lost that connection to that person who is growing and raising that thing for you, that whole exchange is gone except at farmers markets.

Quarterly, we go with our whole staff to see our farmers. Often we will plant the greens for winter in the greenhouse, visit the cows, the sheep, everyone. The idea is that the staff comes back and talks to the customers and everyone feels that old village feel we have lost. The products reinforce that for people. People are amazed that, "This is a bag from a cow I ate last year?? This leather?" Ultimately someone comes in, they eat, and are gone. That sacrifice is lost, but this bag lasts for years. The fact that someone can be remembering that experience and stay connected with that experience for years to come is exciting for us.

Would you say that this is the way forward?

I really think it is. I studied postmodernism and a loss and lack of meaning. I feel that our generation is trying to figure out how to find meaning again. With everyone relying on antidepressants to feel like they want to live their life, there is a resurgence of people growing things, being connected with things, and people just *caring*. Meaning lies in soil, dirt, working, people—all those things.

WORDS AND INTERVIEWS BY SAER RICHARDS

PHOTOGRAPHS BY SETH SMOOT

THE CHEF

At a time where the idea of food as experiment is becoming more prevalent but more isolating, a chef like Sean Rembold is a refreshing comfort. Sean's love of the fundamentals—salt, pepper, and a wooden spoon—make the simple yet ever-changing menu one that is honed so well, it feels as though you are eating the fare of a dear friend who has made the dish all their life.

Why is it important to have a close relationship with your suppliers?

I cannot imagine working in any other manner. For one, it creates a fair exchange of goods. Based on our relationship, we can count on getting the best carrots they can grow. In return we are dedicated to making sure they are paid on time or fronting them money before the season starts, to plant, knowing it will come back on our orders. From a business point it makes sense, but from the creative process, our sous-chefs and I get inspiration in walking into the fridge, tasting a carrot, and saying, "It's amazing." So whereas before you would pair that carrot with other root vegetables or put it in a stew, now we may choose to feature that carrot on its own, because it tastes amazing and can stand on its own. It keeps us in tune with the seasons.

A habit I had to break when I came here is, just because it's Easter doesn't mean that asparagus is ready. You aren't guaranteed to eat asparagus. You have to be patient, you have to wait and then when it arrives you are rewarded with it. Then after a few weeks it's, "Oh, snap peas are ready." Sometimes it requires patience but the payoff is worth it. We end up creating menus that are what people really want to be eating. Whether it's in February when, unfortunately, there aren't a lot of greens so you have to work with your vegetables and salad veg or citrus fruit. It starts to make sense and there is a rhythm to the seasons that is translated to the menus.

Marlow & Sons has quite a small menu. How do you feel it keeps your skills sharp?

I feel we are able to reward our staff, cooks, and myself with a changing menu. It's a lot of problem solving because we are working with a new dish every day we are fine-tuning our skills every day. So a line cook isn't cooking the same dish over and over again and becoming bored to death. They don't know what they are going to be cooking until they come in. You had duck yesterday; today is braised lamb shoulder. We are becoming confident at problem solving whether we realize it or not, and that aides the creative process, as we are confident in knowing what works and what doesn't.

What inspires you?

It's funny to say this but I am most inspired by my staff, my sous-chefs, and I think that's a two-way street. I feel we inspire each other on a daily basis, and it's a family in that sense. I am also inspired by getting to travel occasionally and work with chefs in other cities that are in much different communities and see how they are doing a version of what we are doing. How they are dealing with their farms, or produce or natural wines, or what have you. I think it's something Andrew and I have been trying to implement over the years, where I or my sous-chefs or line cooks go spend time in other cities throughout the year. I feel like chefs in Paris make some amazingly simple but perfect food, and San Francisco is another favorite.

What do you believe is the epitome of good food?

I guess I would say seasonality and seasoning. I think the most important thing is salt and pepper, in the correct amount of seasoning. We love our salt here and sometimes get carried away and it's something we have to teach. I think good food is fresh, it's high quality—whatever it is. Whether it's goose barnacles from Northern Spain, they are amazing.

If the kitchen were on fire, which one tool would you grab?

My sous-chefs. We are all really tight and close friends. I think a wooden spoon is the most valuable kitchen tool just because it doesn't make a lot of loud noise when it hits a pan, so there is a very soothing, calming effect to that. Also, it gets into the corners of the pot so that you don't have things burning down there. It's really the perfect tool. I feel that if you didn't have a knife it's the perfect tool.

WORDS AND INTERVIEWS BY SAER RICHARDS
PHOTOGRAPHS BY SETH SMOOT

CHEESE
ROGUE CREAMERY GOAT/COW (OR)
TWIG FARM GOAT/COW (VT)
RED FURROW F. COW (SCOTLAND)
BOBOLINK CHEDDAR COW (N)
CABOT CHEDDAR COW (VT)

OYSTERS
NAKED COWBOY (NY) 2·75
ST SIMON (NB) 3·00

THE SERVER

Rock 'n' roll may have many sweethearts, but not many are as genuine and inviting as Merica Lee. From the minute she walked into the dining room, it was clear that she was used to engaging with an audience. We are quick to connect, in large part because her smile is fast and her eyes literally sparkle as she talks. It is this genuine ability to connect that makes her role at Marlow & Sons so valuable.

Not only does she connect with patrons on a day-to-day basis, she also uses the considerate ethos of Marlow & Sons to connection with the world on both a personal and a musical level.

What drew you to Marlow & Sons?

I was working at Prune in the city; I went to school with the general manager. It's like Marlow & Sons but maybe a little bit more…Manhattan. I wanted to do a similar thing in Brooklyn where it was looser and cooler.

What do you love most about working here?

There is the element of farm-to-table, local food, and the butcher shop down the road (Marlow & Daughters). I love that we do that and it reminds people this is the way it originally was. It's not bourgeois or for rich people. I like that it keeps that concept edgy and for the common people—it's something that's really important to me. I told the managers if they ever take Budweiser off the list, I'm leaving! We are the Johnny Cash of restaurant people.

What's your most favorite dish?

My mom is Southern so I love disgusting southern food. She makes this thing called SOS—it's like army food from the '40s, sausage and gravy over biscuits.

If the restaurant were on fire, what one thing would you save?

Ooh, I don't know. The top shelf are wines from Andrew's uncle's warehouse, and they were all originally ruined in a fire. The bottles are really old, but being in a fire changed their importance—so maybe a fire is okay. We would just grab the people and build on top.

How important are the people you work with?

It's so family. The great thing about working here is that people stay for a long time because it's so great. I feel I've developed some great friendships with some big characters. We are all treated really well, so we are happy and proud to be here; that's not so common in a restaurant.

It seems as though everyone in Brooklyn is involved in multiple creative projects. What are you working on?

I am in a band with my husband; it's called The Naked Heroes (thenakedheroes.com). I do the drums and he plays guitar and sings. We do a '70s rock 'n' roll thing.

If you could chose anyone to be at your dinner party, who would you want to have attend?

Morrissey, Robert Plant, James Brown—to mix it up a little bit, you know? Cause a bit of trouble! Sinead O'Connor, Lemmy from Motörhead, and Poison Ivy and Lux Interior from The Cramps. I think we would have a really rocking time.

WORDS AND INTERVIEWS BY SAER RICHARDS

PHOTOGRAPHS BY SETH SMOOT

THE RESTAURANT MANAGER

As I sit waiting to chat with John, I am interested by the incredible diversity of the patrons brunching in the dining room of Marlow & Sons. Besides English, the air is filled with the sounds of an intoxicating mix of French, Spanish, and Japanese. Tables are seated with persons ranging from young to retired, locals to out-of-towners. Apparently my presence caught John unawares; he didn't know there was to be an interview this morning. But he is quickly disarmed and speaks fervently and openly about endearing memories of his upbringing in Philadelphia and his hopes for the future, romantic and nostalgic notions that complement his quiet demeanor.

What would you say are the principles of Marlow & Sons?

It's hard to put into words because it's just kind of fun to find this magic. The vibe and atmosphere here is unlike any other place I've been a part of. It starts one hundred percent with the staff; they are really a big reason why people come back and like coming here.

There's a very personal contact here.

We strive for that contact and we try to break the barrier between server and guest.

What would you say inspires you?

My family, with emphasis on my parents. They really taught me what it meant to sit down and break bread with people. We were the type of family that sat down every single night of the week with candles lit, music playing, and no answering the phone during dinnertime. With cell phones it's really hard to do that; I try to keep mine turned off when I sit down to eat.

I also feel kind of lucky that the people I work with are a huge inspiration to me every day. From the owners to the last employee they are all fantastic people to be around, which makes it easy to work with and be a part of this family.

What makes everyone so great?

Your guess is as good as mine; it's that magic again. We genuinely enjoy showing hospitality and showing people a good time, and we enjoy each other's company in doing that, in providing that service to people. And we like to have a good laugh—that's huge.

What book are you reading right now?

I'm reading—a couple of us are reading—*The Third Reich* by Roberto Bolaño. He died in 2003 and this was among his papers; they are publishing it in four parts in *The Paris Review*. We are kind of all passing around our copies and are all sitting on our hands waiting for the final installment.

What projects do you working on in your free time?

One thing, I'm on the search for the perfect sour beer—it's brewed with wild yeast and is such a pervasive process, a brewery has to practically give themselves up to brewing only that type of beer. We actually carry a few here at Marlow & Sons: Cantillon Classic Gueuze and Cantillon Rosé de Gambrinus. Also, Hanssen›s Oude Gueuze. And we have other sour beers that aren›t classified as Lambics, like Dr. Fritz Briem 1809 Berliner Style Weisse, which is a wheat beer made with lactic acid bacteria; it›s pretty tart.

What's next for you?

I have this romantic idea of moving to Pittsburgh, which is where my dad and mom are from. It's weird, it's sort of like I have nostalgia for it because I grew up going there but I never really lived there and I don't know the city that well. It's like reverse nostalgia—like nostalgia for the future.

It's definitely a romantic notion.

It's a romantic idea. My Gran still lives there I have a couple of uncles there as well; it's an amazing city but I haven't had it with Brooklyn yet, and I'm not sure if I will be soon.

Brooklyn is a tough place to leave.

It's an amazing place for sure.

What is it that Brooklyn has?

At the moment it has a very vibrant scene of do-it-yourselfers, which is fairly unique. But aside from that, I think what it has that makes it a spectacular place is the amount of culture—it's incredible. If you cross the street you have one of the biggest Hasidic neighborhoods; we are sharing this area, this space with so many people. It's incredible.

WORDS AND INTERVIEWS BY SAER RICHARDS

PHOTOGRAPHS BY SETH SMOOT

THE MERCANTILE MANAGER

When you speak with Sara Moffat, you can't help being drawn in by her passion for locally made, everyday goods. Having owned a clothing line for seven years with design partner Teo Griscom, Sara has a hands-on-approach that is reflected in the way she manages the Marlow & Sons store. The shop bustles with an eclectic yet cohesive mix of locally made brands and intriguing European imports. It is with a similar eclecticism that Sara lives. Her personal website www.saramoffat.com serves as evidence of an ever-growing roster of talent from artist to designer to stylist—and more.

Your clothing line, jjr, was developed through a very meticulous process. How has that influenced what you are doing here?

It's along the same lines; I won't buy anything made in China. We are this cool, unique place that people come to. For several years, I've been meeting people doing small production—really sustainable, well-minded stuff. One thing I started looking for was wooden spoons. I was trying to go so many ways with this. I tried to find antique spoons, and my antique source goes, "There's this great guy I found who's a tree trimmer and on the side he makes, as his passion, spoons from tree trunks." So I contacted him and I was like, "Can you make spoons? But make them smaller than usual?" And now we have spoons. We also have socks from the wool from the sheep farm in Maine.

The idea is to work seasonally—work it like a general store, where you can get the goods you need in their season. Whether it's wool socks or a pair of shoes, a beach basket or sunscreen, you can get them knowing that everything is not a random choice.

Is a background story to the products you sell important to you?

Yes absolutely. So I try and educate the staff to be able to reference all the stories. We have jump ropes made by a woman who makes dog leashes—she lives down the street. Our favorite house care products, laundry soap, hand soap, and dish soap are also made by a woman down the street.

I get to explore as much as I can. We have things from France: for example, we have always carried Armor Lux. The owner speaks French so she was able to order it over the phone.

Do you see yourself as setting a standard locally?

I think if that happens it's not intentional. I try to have an awareness of what the neighborhood needs, what will sell, and some of it is risk-taking and seeing that taking off. Kate can tell you about her bags; the leather is from the skins of the animals we serve here. So in the mercantile, instead of meat being on that meat rack, it's a bag.

How do you feel your upbringing influenced what you do today?

My parents moved to a local organic commune in Colorado when I was two. It was really cool. We stayed on a few years and were associated with them for several years after. It got a little weird in the '80s, but we then moved back to the woods in Colorado and raised chickens, grew apples, grazed all our food. It was there that I learned about herbs. My dad was a landscape artist so he was always growing plants. I had a knack for that like, "Oh you have a bee sting? You put this on it and chew it up and spit it on there."

Who are your three go-to brands or designers?

Breton: That is Kate's label that she's been using to make the leather bags.

jackson, johnston & roe: We've always carried that label and are going to continue to carry the aprons.

Armor Lux: It's been here for years and years.

What's next?

Setting up the website for retail with the help of Chris and Maria (More & Co.), which is so great because a lot of times people come in and are like, "I want that bag! Let me get that bag! I love that bag but have to go back to England!" So it's very exciting for us to soon be able to provide the bags for people all over.

WORDS AND INTERVIEWS BY SAER RICHARDS

PHOTOGRAPHS BY SETH SMOOT

THE BARISTA

The smell of coffee that permeates the store and café space is both comforting and addicting. The rather long, yet patient, line that snakes through the space seems to agree. If coffee were an artist's palette, Heather would be a most careful and thoughtful painter. She has honed the skill since her teen years, and now her role as barista is, in her eyes, part of "creating a conversation": cafés are a universal meeting place, and somewhere that people want to feel comfortable to open up and talk. Facilitating that process is as important to her as making the best possible cup.

Where are you from originally?

I grew up in a suburb of Chicago, thirty miles west of the city. At seventeen I moved to Chicago and lived there for a few years, and then wanted to get out of the Midwest, so moved to Seattle. Lived there a couple years, then to San Francisco for a couple, then back to Seattle, then to New York two years ago.

How did you become a barista?

At the end of high school I got a job at Starbucks, and that was the beginning of learning a new skill set. When I moved out of the suburb I was in, I quit Starbucks because it was so corporate. It was nice for insurance and stuff like that, but now I had this particular kind of skill—being a barista. It's not difficult but it's definitely a set of skills that not everyone has.

It's easy to get different jobs in different cafés so I scouted out locations of cafés that I liked and wanted to work at, places I thought would be good for me, and places I'd want to meet people and talk to people. I just went from there, and I've had café jobs since then.

What's the best coffee you have tasted?

There are two answers to that. Because there is one that comes to mind, but I haven't tasted it in some years so it might have changed. The best now, currently in Brooklyn, are the ones I make for myself [laughs]. But no, I love the coffee here; we feature a bunch of different types of espresso.

A new coffee company is Handsome Coffee Roasters; they are out of LA. They are fairly new I think and I really like them—I like what they are doing with their roast. They make an espresso blend that we sell. I also love Blue Bottle Coffee, which is here in Brooklyn. But the first thought that came to mind was in 2004, when I moved to Seattle, I went to Vivace. They had the best espresso that I've ever tasted, in my memory. Though now they may have changed, but when I tried them that was a new beginning for me.

What would you say are the three key elements of your job?

Quality: Quality control of what you are making and serving. That's important.

Customer Service: Giving people what they want, and happily. Working with them to find out what they want.

Creating A Conversation: Creating a homey environment, especially with coffee. Cafés are very much a meeting place; it's like people get together to get a cup of coffee and talk and this is a space people feel comfortable doing that.

What are your sources of inspiration?

Nature is a big one for me; I leave the city a lot. I have a car, so I go to the country and take my dog; we go for hikes. We just went upstate, around the Jeffersonville area. I know this because my dog got poked by a porcupine and I had to take him to a vet. He stung his nose. It was beautiful though—he looked tough, like a total punk with tons of spikes sticking out of his face! I'm not an avid hiker; I just like to go out and go for walks. I have friends who live in Western Massachusetts, so I like to go there. Vermont. There are little places I try to go every couple weeks.

Being in NYC, there is so much going on. So at the same time as nature, the city. I'm really into architecture. I live on a street of brownstones, I love the brownstones. Any time of year they are beautiful, you walk down the street in the middle of the winter and you're cold, and snow's coming down, and they are beautiful. I used to be inspired by industrial-type buildings as they're so fluid. But I am very into the country cabin aesthetic with antlers. I have a lot of skulls at home. Some I've gotten from the butcher shop, ducks, deer, goat, a bobcat. The bobcat, a friend bought from San Francisco. I have a bunch of them. It's nice, in the city, to have that surrounding me. I feel more in tune with nature.

WORDS AND INTERVIEWS BY SAER RICHARDS

PHOTOGRAPHS BY SETH SMOOT

Marlow & Sons restores hope. Hope in the will of people to take a careful approach to life,
to care about where one's goods come from, and to be conscious of using resources to their fullest.
Hope that by using simple ingredients and using them well, a back-to-basics approach to life will be bred.
And even more so, hope that these things will one day be viewed as the norm and not the exceptional.

SAER RICHARDS

SMITH TOWER

A PHOTO ESSAY BY KYLE JOHNSON
STYLING BY ASHLEY HELVEY
COOKING BY MOLLY WIZENBERG AND BRANDON PETTIT

*Ambiance is essential to entertaining: the mood and energy that your friends will feel,
the atmosphere that dictates the flow of interaction and conversation. If you' need of a change of pace,
opt for a simple venue change. Skip the decorations; try a picnic at a park, a beach soirée, or a meal on a rooftop.
The novelty and intrigue of the new surroundings will invigorate and enliven a casual gathering,
providing its own natural and unforgettable ambiance.*

ON THE ROAD / OFF THE GRID

A COUPLE RECONNECTS BY UNPLUGGING AND HITTING THE OPEN ROAD

PHOTOGRAPHS BY JENNIFER CAUSEY AND LILY STOCKMAN

WORDS BY LILY STOCKMAN

We were the only people for miles. No phones, no computers, no television.

N ice little Scamp trailer. 1978. Fully carpeted. *Good condition.* That's all the Craigslist ad said, and it was all we needed to know. We made an offer before Gino, the owner of the Scamp, had even unlocked the powder-blue fiberglass door.

Gino was a retired Sicilian airline pilot, spry in his early eighties, and debonair with a silver moustache like fountain pen nibs and a pompadour to make Little Richard blush. My husband Peter and I had, over the course of the weekend, decided that what we really needed in our lives was a vintage fiberglass travel trailer. And after a few hours on Craigslist, we found ourselves in a barbwire-ensconced parking lot behind the Bel Aire Mobile Estates, writing a check for two thousand dollars to one Gino Romanelli for one 1978 Scamp (fully carpeted, good condition, as promised).

We laughed the whole drive home, giddy at the lunacy of spending our tax return on such a frivolous lark. But I awoke the next morning with a butter churn of regret in my gut. There in our driveway sat a thirteen-by-eight-foot fiberglass egg, like some retro space capsule whose Soviet crew had mistaken our Joshua Tree, California, driveway for a Martian landing pad. Our grand plans for a summer adventure suddenly seemed more Regretsy than *Blue Highways*.

Let's back up a little. Peter and I had been married for less than a year before his Marine unit shipped off to Iraq. And just like that, my sweetheart evaporated into the ether of a distant war. Peter and I Skyped when he had internet access near Fallujah, and I'd run around pointing my laptop camera to the wagging dogs, the hummingbirds at the feeder, the electric haze of spring wildflowers carpeting the desert floor. Sometimes it was so painful I closed my eyes to just concentrate on his voice; it made him seem closer, somehow, when I wasn't looking at the pixilated delay of his sunburnt, wind-chapped face. Ours was an e-marriage, a long-distance romance of silence and worry punctuated by brief and euphoric online exchanges that, when over, brought severe bouts of sadness. It was heartbreaking.

And so when Peter returned we made a pact. We would unplug our marriage and take some time to be, as one friend put it, "present, together." His active duty contract was about to expire (the Marines had paid his college tuition

and in return he owed four years of active duty service) and we had big decisions to make about our next step. We applied for grants and secured arrangements that would allow for us to live and study in India for one year, but in the meantime we had the summer free. Which was exactly what we needed. We had spent more time apart in our fledgling marriage than we had together, and we were desperate for time to reconnect.

But before we moved halfway across the globe, we wanted to see America. I had never seen Mount Rushmore. Peter had never seen the Grand Canyon. And, let's be honest, neither of us had ever seen the Mitchell Corn Palace. So we bought the Scamp for two reasons: one, to put some sweat equity into a tangible project together, and two, to have the welcome-back-from-war-let's-have-some-fun road trip of a lifetime.

However. When push came to shove, neither of us really knew what "restoring" the Scamp actually entailed. Over a Saturday morning cup of coffee we peered around the corner of our house at the gleaming marshmallow parked in our driveway, plotting our plan of attack as if about to ambush a cantankerous rhinoceros. It was decided the best course of action was to rip out all the junk and see what lay beneath Gino's enthusiastic late-70s décor choices. Get down the bones of the beast, if you will.

You really had to hand it to Gino: the interior was remarkable. It looked like a guest room at Graceland and smelled like a disco club. Out came yard after yard of tiger-striped polyester carpeting, which he'd spray-glued to the floor, walls, and ceiling like the plush interior of some nightmarish, oversized Fabergé egg. We dismantled the tiny cabinet doors, which were covered in an especially ghastly cerulean crushed velvet. The collection of vintage *RV America* VHS tapes, the macramé throw pillows, and the brown-and-orange polyester blanket went to the Joshua Tree Salvation Army. But after that, we were clueless about what to do next.

There's that moment in every respectable adventure odyssey when the protagonist loses her way, and she goes about seeking council from the mountaintop sage with all the answers. Our Scamp restoration odyssey was no different. So into the Google search bar I typed "restoring vintage Scamp trailer," and lo and behold, a world

*Everyone in our virtual world, it seemed, was eager to build a tiny kingdom on wheels,
leave the stresses of regular life behind, and hit the open road.*

of *Dwell*-worthy fiberglass dreams flashed across my computer screen. Which is to say that in order to unplug from the computer and embark on an epic journey in the wilderness, one must first embark on an epic journey on the computer.

And so the real restoration work began in earnest. We stayed up late each night poring through online accounts of trial-by-fire restoration projects; Flickr, Facebook, Tumblr, blogs, the forums on fiberglassRV.com—we trawled them all. We found strangers willing to email us advice on voltage converters, flexible flooring models, and even specific brands of fiberglass touch-up paint. We discovered an online community of information swappers, do-it-yourselfers, advice givers and, like any group of eccentric hobbyists, the delightfully fervid warring factions within. There was the Scamp vs. Airstream debate (roadies vs. retirees), fiberglass vs. steel body (Prius-driving weekend warriors vs. F250 Super Duty-driving snowbirds), thirteen footer vs. twenty-six footer (solo minimalists vs. Edward Sharpe & the Magnetic Zeros), and of course the no-toilet die-hards vs. everyone else.

And then there was us: two late-twenty-somethings, one an artist, the other an infantry Marine, trying to spend some quality time together. We didn't exactly fit the profile of your average Scamp owner (retired, Canadian, dehydrates own jerky), but we ragtag tribe of travel trailer enthusiasts were all in it for the same reasons. Everyone in our virtual world, it seemed, was eager to build a tiny kingdom on wheels, leave the stresses of regular life behind, and hit the open road.

Let me crow, if you'll indulge me for a moment, about the merits of the Scamp. Le Château de Scamp is unique in that it's so lightweight you can drive into the middle of nowhere, unhitch it from your vehicle, and wheel it like a giant igloo-to-go into your camping spot of choice. Inside, the dinette has a proper two-burner propane stove, a wee sink with an ingenious Peter-designed cutting board cover, a table that folds down into a perfectly acceptable bed (thanks to a two-inch-thick memory foam mattress), and room to spare for two dogs on the floor. It's essentially a dollhouse for mildly insane grown-ups.

Our goal was to drive a little every day, see the National Parks, read a lot of books, and sleep in beautiful, pristine wilderness. And with

a Scamp, one needs not the amenities of hotels and roadside restaurants; the Scamp is the perfect mobile living device, minus the mobile devices. No laptops allowed (ok, occasional Internetting allowed on "town days"). The point was to unplug and unwind, *together*.

Three months after handing our check over to Gino (Gino, Gino, we will never forget Gino), the Scamp boasted brand new power converters, sink plumbing, reupholstered cushions, dinette table, screen door, faux bamboo floor, chrome fixtures, and freshly painted cabinets and interior. She gleamed from the outside, but inside she positively sparkled.

We put all our belongings in storage save for a duffel bag of clothes for our year in India, several crates of books, two fresh loaves of desert sourdough from our neighbors, a bottle of good bourbon, and a twenty-pound bag of dog food. We spent the first night of our Great American Road Trip just two miles away, tucked among the monzogranite rock formations in Joshua Tree National Park.

Peter stacked kindling and got a good bonfire going. The flickering light caught ribbons of quartz in the boulders, which shimmered and twinkled like distant constellations. I opened up the bourbon and heated a can of soup on the petite Scamp stove, admiring the new propane valve control Peter had so expertly installed thanks to Vince P.'s tutorial on Flickr. Our two dogs lay contentedly by the fire, pricking their ears when the coyotes took up their nighttime chorus. We were the only people for miles. No phones, no computers, no television. I brought the soup outside and sat down next to this man I loved, this man who bought a beat-up old travel trailer to amuse his wife, this man who lovingly restored it so they could go Scamping together. Above us, the full moon was an egg yolk in the desert sky, and around us, the galaxy and the desert were one seamless, velvet expanse of possibilities.

"You know what?" Peter asked as he took his first spoonful of soup. I turned to face my husband.

"This is just the beginning."

Lily Stockman is a Brooklyn-based artist, adjunct professor of painting at NYU, and author of the blog bigBANG studio. She and her husband Peter remain devoted Scamp enthusiasts. ○

MAMA'S SOUP

Memory, coupled with taste, is a powerful thing. One of my most vivid childhood memories is of my mother stirring a pot of what my brother and I dubbed "Mama's soup" while we sat at the counter waiting expectantly for the first bowl. While the chicken broth—a golden homemade concoction of bones and root vegetables—bubbled on a back burner, my mother would sauté shredded carrots and onions together until sweet and caramelized. These would go into the strained broth with cauliflower, parsnips, potatoes, a handful of pastina, and chopped dill. Small matzo balls, not relegated to Hanukkah in our household, were the finishing touch.

This one-pot meal was what sustained us for years, through blustery winters and cool summer evenings. It is the Jewish version of minestrone, a humble peasant-style soup, a soup that can be eaten with a hunk of buttered bread or some boiled potatoes and herring, a nod to our Russian-Jewish heritage. It is a soup that will leave you asking for seconds and thirds.

I spent countless hours sitting at the kitchen counter, a steaming soup bowl in front of me, discussing my homework or my tennis match with my parents. Decisions, from what college to attend to what academic endeavor to pursue, were discussed over spoon and bowl. My attempts to recreate my mother's recipe have come from necessity—I don't live near home—and generally involve multiple telephone calls and burned carrots. I often think it would be easier to make the long drive from my apartment in Brooklyn to my parents' house in upstate New York, if only to recreate the magic of arriving home knowing my mother will be waiting for me with ladle in hand.

In a recent visit, I watched her spooning soup into my two-year-old niece's mouth, whose chubby cheeks were rosy from the steam of the soup, while my mother's were flushed from the joy of feeding her grandchild and hearing her ask, "More soup please." Rewind twenty-five years and the exact same image of myself and my *babushka* flashes through my mind. My grandmother's greatest pleasure was to feed her family, particularly her grandchildren. My brother and I would walk into her home and immediately she would begin emptying the contents of her refrigerator onto the table. Any attempt to dissuade her or claim we weren't hungry fell on deaf ears. The thought of unfinished or wasted food was a travesty to my grandmother, largely due to years of scarce supplies and long lines in the Soviet Union.

Fortunately we don't have to wait in line for chicken or vegetables anymore. The recipe that was stretched to feed a family of four for days is no longer a recipe of necessity but of nostalgia and memory. My brother's children are the next generation of Mama's soup devotees, slurping up broth and matzo balls while reciting the events of their day. This soup is my mother's legacy, a tribute to her heritage and the love she bestows on all of us, through the kitchen.

WORDS BY AGATHA KHISHCHENKO
PHOTOGRAPH BY HEATHER NAN

OFFICE HYGGE

Everything that bothered me about the forced lunch scheme melted away when
I tasted food that was made with love, even though it came from a work canteen.

One of the toughest and most time-consuming parts of our workday is the lunch debate. No matter what workplace you are in, it's part of the conversation. In my experience, the best lunch break is when you actually share a moment with your colleagues, with only a few simple ingredients: people, food, and the knowledge you have a set window of time in which to enjoy it all.

I am originally from Canada, and I am accustomed to eating lunch while trying to reply to ten emails, read an article, and design the next photo shoot at the same time. In my opinion, this kind of multitasking links to the TV-dinner culture and is best avoided. The custom of taking the lunch hour for myself was thrown out the window when I moved to Europe and was introduced to—as it was itemized on my salary—the "Danish Lunch Scheme." It was no longer up to me what I ate or when I ate it, and I was forced to socialize with my co-workers. This resulted in feelings of anxiety and irritation, which were soon replaced by satisfaction and calm. My food intake was no longer a concern, which gave me more time to focus on the job at hand and the opportunity to bond with my colleagues in a whole new way. This is the Danish style of doing things, and is part of an elusive and confusing concept known as *hygge*.

Hygge is a fundamental aspect of Danish culture. Although I dare not define it, one possible description would be: spending a calm, cozy time with loved ones, often while enjoying good food and drink. This doesn't come close to fully explaining the term, nor what it felt like experiencing it. Everything that bothered me about the forced lunch scheme melted away when I tasted food that was made with love, even though it came from a work canteen. On my first day working in Copenhagen, the menu included a rack of lamb, fresh seasonal cherries, and rich chocolate cake

for dessert. I savored the tastes and traditions—familiar to so many—with each delicious bite.

Living in Scandinavia certainly has its moments, but it's impressive to witness how the people wholeheartedly embrace the simple pleasures in life, in order to make long winters bearable and to eventually soak up the brilliant summer light. I soon became a lover of winter bathing; I learned that the simple addition of candlelight can completely transform a room; I tasted simple food that oozed with the chef's love. Having relocated, with no family or friends in Denmark, it was hard to imagine that a few months in I would be exposed to so many traditions that involved eating, drinking, and socializing.

After years of enjoying many beautiful aspects of Copenhagen, I recently moved to New York. I was welcomed into Mucca, an award-winning firm made up of international designers and located in the busy Soho district. I eagerly anticipated the traditions these New Yorkers would be able to share with me.

Bringing *hygge* to Soho was no easy feat. The rules I set for myself were to source ingredients locally, deliver on my bicycle, and stick to a budget. Ideally, a company will foster a lunch scheme; however when this isn't the case, creative solutions are necessary.

These staples make small bites that don't feel like take-away. Treating your taste buds to fresh fare, as opposed to food wrapped in cellophane, is one step toward achieving *hygge* in New York City.

SIMPLE SOLUTIONS

Good-quality staples for the office pantry: Salt and pepper, Olive oil, Citrus fruits, Honey

Staples for the office refrigerator: Yogurt, Bread or crisp bread (for easy storage), Greens, Cured meat and fish, Cheese, Seasonal fruits and vegetables

WORDS AND ART DIRECTION BY LYNSAY REYNOLDS
PHOTOGRAPHS BY JENNIFER CAUSEY

CALIFORNIA RETREAT

WORDS BY SHAUNNA NYGREN

PHOTOGRAPHS BY ASHLEY CAMPER

We were looking to be inspired by nature, the new and the unknown.

When friends are scattered across the earth, it can take an alluring adventure to bring them all together. The romance of the open road and Northern California's rugged coastline was the ticket this time. We were looking to be inspired by nature, the new and the unknown. It was a modest attempt at rediscovering America's quaint, picturesque seaside towns of a bygone era. Northern California is one riveting mix of freethinkers, vintners, farmers, surfers, home-brewers, underground diners, and intellects. We packed light for our journey: woven blankets, sweaters, and our favorite records.

Kicking off the voyage, we spent a hazy afternoon at Scribe Winery in Sonoma, roaming the wild grounds and exploring the beautifully distressed Mission Revival Style hacienda. There are treasures to unearth around every bend: Prohibition-era glass bottles, tattered books, poetry etched on the walls—vintage everything, basically. The Scribe experience is rich in rebel history, debonair taste, and natural splendor. From there, we called a picnic table home at Hog Island Oyster Farm, mastering the delicate art of shucking oysters. Brackish rivers flow into the salty Pacific Ocean. We breathed in Tomales Bay then hit the road, opting for the scenic route along California's Highway 1. There is nothing quite like old friends and great adventures, drinking in the freedom of the open road.

Santa Cruz lured us in with its ease of life and famed surf culture. At dusk, we strolled the boardwalk for a dose of pure nostalgia. Our gaze landed on the most awe-inducing landscape. Vivid hues of melon yellow and gold punctuated the sky in Big Sur. Much like exploring Maui's road to Hana, traveling to this California hamlet was about the journey, not the destination.

With every end of the road, I think of Colette's words penned in *The Vagabond,* "It is true that departures sadden and exhilarate me, and whatever I pass through—new countries, skies pure or cloudy, seas under rain the colour of a grey pearl—something of myself catches on it and clings so passionately that I feel as though I were leaving behind me a thousand little phantoms in my image, rocked on the waves, cradled in the leaves, scattered among the clouds." [3] ○

COURT STREET GROCERS

We sat together in the cozy restaurant
with no pretense beyond sharing a table, sharing a meal.

I read an interesting statistic a few days ago: if the state of Texas was as densely populated as New York City, it could accommodate the entire world's population.

As a recent transplant from the former to the latter, I often feel torn about which extreme I prefer. On the one hand, it is hard not to feel moved by urban energy; I often describe living in New York City as simply "intense," which can be a good thing. On the other hand, sometimes I wish I had a little more space to just *be*—away from the continual, palpable awareness of my presence in a crowd.

City life necessitates many small interactions with strangers. I walk with them on the street; I sit next to them on the subway; I stand behind them in line to buy a morning coffee. But despite nearly living on top of them, I rarely interact with people I don't know. What's more, I feel as though I barely register them at all. This isn't for lack of curiosity—I wonder about their jobs, whether they order sparkling or tap, if they have any recommendations for places to develop film. However, I keep to myself as a survival tactic, as a way of maintaining my emotional armor. I subconsciously block out the millions of foreign lives around me so I don't have to feel their weight. Instead, I seek solace in my book, or from my headphones. As

Melissa Febos recently wrote in a *New York Times* Opinionator blog post, "In a place where we are so rarely alone, we find privacy in public." [2]

—

At the onset of autumn, I gathered with six others for a dinner that began as a way to celebrate the emerging fall produce and ended as a lesson in the value of unfamiliarity.

The setting was the dining room of Court Street Grocers, a perfect little market-*cum*-café in Brooklyn's Carroll Gardens neighborhood. Aside from my boyfriend, Michael, and one of his friends who happened to live down the street, we were a group of strangers essentially bound by our relative proximity and the weird power of the Internet. We sat together in the cozy restaurant with no pretense beyond sharing a table, sharing a meal. And what stays in my memory about the night is not the specific conversations, or the types of cheese we were served—to be honest, many details escape me. What remains is the surprising power that came from spending a few hours in the company of unfamiliar faces, the reminder that what is to be gained out of gathering is not just feeling comfortable. Rather, it is something more simple and quite humbling: New York is big, but my own personal New York is so small. Sometimes I need a little perspective.

WORDS BY LEIGH PATTERSON
PHOTOGRAPHS BY MICHAEL MULLER

BECOMING A HOME

There we were so far from what we generically called home,
and when we left, we left another home we've built...

Home away from home. I've said it about so many places. Not just said it, though, but really *felt* it. I love home so much—my home, the place I live, with my family, with my memories, with all the things that feel comfortable and, well, homey. And whenever I'm away from home, I miss that place. That home-place. Yet I have this terribly beautiful habit of making the away-place become a home. It's almost accidental. It's one of those habits that's subconscious, like playing with my hair when I'm nervous—when I realize I've done it, it's too late to pretend I haven't.

We spent seven weeks in a little village in Uganda during the autumn. At home, the leaves were bursting into flames, changing into something that is divine because it lasts for but a breath. In Uganda there is rain and sun. Two seasons. While I missed the autumnal symphony at home, something like it happened in our family. We went from two to three during those seven weeks. The change is but a breath, but the growing will keep growing. Age is a crown of glory, I've heard. I can see that in the trees.

I always wonder when it happens—when the away-place reminds me of home. It was already happening in Uganda, from many previous visits. This time was particularly unique as it brought our family together for the first time in fifteen months, establishing a bond that had begun four years before. I wonder if women feel this way about the room they give birth in. Seven weeks isn't very long, it really isn't, but neither is seven hours of labor. Sometimes the emotion, energy, and expectation make time stop, and you can't count it anymore.

We woke up every morning to metal clanking on metal as a line of children pumped water at the borehole. I waited for tea water to boil and watched the children laughing and playing as they waited—for their turn to pump and for the sun to rise. Some of them were quieter, and I thought about how I'd be among them, wrapped up in a towel, still waking up. After the sun rose, we walked to the market. We picked produce from the same lady every day, and we knew we were accepted when she started giving us the "local" price, instead of adding on the extra cents here and there. We used the produce to make a dinner and tried to finish before the power went out—it was always a battle against the power. At first, all these things felt inconvenient and uncomfortable. I may have grumbled about bathing out of a bucket, at first. But soon, it just became normal. Traditional. A routine.

In just a few weeks we had found our favorites: the best spot to drink our coffee in the morning, where the freshest and cheapest eggs were, the town an hour away that was perfect to get away on the weekends, the best bowl of curry in the country. So by the end of seven weeks, we were friends with the regular patrons of these favorites, and friends with the staff, and in seven weeks we somehow managed to become regulars—we were being asked if we wanted the usual.

I think this isn't just my habit. I think we all have it. We are humans and we live. We can't help it. There we were so far from what we generically called home, and when we left, we left another home we've built, another home to tuck away in a neighborhood in our mind, next to all the rest. And each home, no matter how temporary, is so heartbreakingly sweet.

PHOTOGRAPHS AND WORDS BY CARISSA GALLO

THE MANLY HOST

A NEW SERIES OF COLLECTIONS

A PHOTO ESSAY BY GENTL & HYERS

1. AN EVENING WHITTLE

2. SATURDAY MORNING PANCAKES

3. MIDDAY ROAST

4. GAME NIGHT

VOLUME THREE CREDITS

SPECIAL THANKS
Paintings Katie Stratton
Art Director at Weldon Owen Ali Zeigler
Production Director at Weldon Owen Chris Hemesath

COVER PHOTO
Photographer Seth Smoot

BACK COVER QUOTE
Wendell Berry, *The Long-Legged House* (Washington,
DC: Shoemaker & Hoard, 2004), 61.

CLOSING PAINTING
Artist Katie Stratton

ENDNOTES
1 Rainer Maria Rilke, *Letters to a Young Poet*, trans.
Stephen Mitchell (Random House, 1984), 36-7.

2 Melissa Febos, "Look at Me, I'm Crying."
Opinionator (blog), *New York Times*, April
20, 2011, http://opinionator.blogs.nytimes.
com/2011/04/20/look-at-me-im-crying/.

3 Colette, *The Vagabond*, trans. Enid McLeod
(New York: Farrar, Straus and Young, 1955), 74.

THE MANLY HOST
White pot Baum-Kuchen
www.baum-kuchen.net

Chocolate Mast Brothers & Olive and Sinclair
www.mastbrothers.com
www.oliveandsinclair.blogspot.com

WWW.KINFOLKMAG.COM

KEEP IN TOUCH